I pray God's
clearest
voice over
you as you
seek His
direction in
life.

the
blAck girl's
guide to living on purpose

Here's to purposeful
living,

brie daniels

this book belongs to:

_____

Cover Design by Dudley C. Grady Jr.

ISBN-13: 978-1522996880
ISBN-10: 1522996885

I dedicate this book to all of my Level VI: XII babies (yes I know you're teens, technically). Working with you in ministry has opened up so many doors for me and confirmed that I'm exactly where I'm supposed to be.

Acknowledgements

I would be remiss not to thank the following people for their assistance with this project. First, giving glory to God for talking me through this process. Whether speaking directly to me or through a friend, He always provided the encouragement I needed.

To my editor Karen Celestan for her honesty about what changes were critical to this piece. To Kemberley Washington for inspiring me and answering all my questions about being an author. Just seeing you walk in your gift has blessed me.

To Justin McCain for helping me solidify my decision to self-publish. To Lila Blanchard for inspiring me to understand what worship means to me. To Candace Bolden, Zuri Gracin and Miyah Davis for reading my first draft and critiquing it. To Dudley C. Grady Jr. for my awesome cover design. To Alyson Nicholas who kept me company during the editing process. To my husband Geordan for your love, encouragement, goofiness and patience.

Finally, to my parents, my sister, and all my friends who supported this, your confidence in me helped me fight to the finish.

Contents

Then Jesus spoke to them again: *"I am the light of the world. Anyone who follows Me will never walk in darkness but will have the light of life."*
John 8:12, HCSB

Introduction

God gave me the title for *The Black Girl's Guide to Living on Purpose* before He gave me the content and I couldn't really understand why He wanted me to be that specific. I felt like I was setting myself up for the "black lives matter" versus "all lives matter" debate again.

That was before October 27, 2015 when while browsing my Facebook news feed, I saw a video of a teenage girl who was thrown from her desk and body slammed for so-called class "disruption."[1]

As I watched that video, I immediately understood that while this book is applicable to girls of all ethnicities, I specifically need my black and brown young ladies to understand the value of purposeful living because in the age we're in, it's highly likely that you will see videos and images that deem your life worthless or void of purpose.

You will read comments from people who defend the actions of police officers and teachers abusing their positions. You will read about students at the University of Missouri, who were threatened just because they pushed for better policies and called for the resignation of a university president who did not seem to care about their condition.[2] You will read about how one woman who did not signal a lane change wound up in police custody and subsequently died.[3] You may even stumble across the articles reporting that black girls are six times more likely to be suspended than their white counterparts[4] resulting in more black girls being funneled into the school-to-prison pipeline.

These striking realities make it extremely critical for you to realize, no matter what you read or see on TV, you have to keep on living. You must know how important your existence is and decide within yourself that you will live your life on purpose. When you have the right foundation you can stand upon the fact that God is in control and He always has a plan even when the world around you is set on sinking sand.

As you continue to live as a young woman who understands her purpose for living, you will forge ahead with the kind of determination that refuses to be shaken no matter what lies ahead.

Be encouraged dear, you are about to enter a new phase of living.

Preface

Have you ever had a moment when you looked around and wondered "What am I here for?" or felt, even for an instant, that your life was insignificant? Believe it or not, that's not uncommon. Everyone on this Earth has asked or will ask at some point, "What is my purpose?" Sadly, not everyone will consult the right sources.

I remember when I first started to inquire about my significance on this planet. I fumbled around in high school and college, trying to grab hold of anything to give my life meaning. I often looked to friendships or guys I "dated" casually (I put the quotation marks because I believe everyone I met before Geordan was a simple interaction on my way to a relationship with true meaning). I thought that other people could provide my validity, that in them I would discover some deeper meaning for everything. In the end, because they are human like me, seeking the approval of other individuals just led to an empty feeling.

I do not want that to be your story. I want you to be able to consult the Source who provides everything you need. His name is God, in the form of The Father, Christ the Son and the Holy Spirit. I promise that once you get linked up with Him and allow Him to be the One from Whom you seek direction, the life you have will start to make a lot more sense and you will become more intentional with it. As you make new discoveries, you will find yourself greeting each day with the expectation of huge opportunities. God will allow demonstrate them through your ministry. He will reveal your talents and gifts and He will give you strength and direction as you dedicate yourself daily to purposeful living. This is a critical principle to me, as I have seen the way finding purpose helps fight feelings of inferiority, combat thoughts that you don't matter and avoid confusion about why you were created.

In this book, I plan to share some changes I made that helped me in my search for purpose. We will talk about where you should start when trying to find your purpose. Spoiler alert: it's with God. We will, among other things, spend some time discovering your spiritual gifts and passions, discussing the importance of establishing the kinds of friendships that will keep you on your path to purpose and what to do once you have found it.

Each chapter combines my experiences with biblical teaching. I was intentional in doing this because without sound doctrine, this book would just be a collection of personal stories. I want to set you up for things that will follow you to eternity. One person's circumstances can vary from day to day, but God's Word is unchanging.

You will notice that I use a lot of shorthand like NLT, HCSB, NASB after scripture readings. These letters outline the Bible version I am citing. You will see the Holman Christian Standard Bible (HCSB), New Living Translation (NLT), the Message Bible (The Message), the English Standard Version (ESV) and the New American Standard Bible (NASB) translations. I've chosen this variety based on what I felt would be helpful and easy to comprehend during Bible study. At the end of each chapter, you'll find a list of action steps to help you apply everything we discuss. I challenge you to read one chapter a day so you can really allow the principles I am sharing to dig deep. If you are like me and love going the extra mile, consider keeping a journal to write out your thoughts as you undergo this purpose-seeking process. The time for purposeful living is now. Let's get started.

Part 1:

Prepared for your Purpose

"For which of you, wanting to build a tower, does not first sit down and calculate the cost to see if he has enough to complete it?"
Luke 14:28 (HCSB)

My family took a lot of road trips when my sister and I were younger. We drove to Orlando, San Antonio, Galveston, Atlanta, Columbia and it's because of all these trips, that I love being on the road so much today. There is something really special about wide open space with and few distractions but I digress.

Before each trip my dad would get the car serviced: get an oil change, have the tires rotated and fill up the gas tank. He wanted to make sure the car was prepared to go the distance and never wanted us to get stuck on the side of the road because he had not properly prepared, he had not gotten a proper assessment.

Your life deserves the same if not more attention. If you're going to finish the race of life (Philippians 3:14) then you have to go through a preparation process.

You have to take time to observe what you are good at, to see how your personality ties into the personalities of those around you, to discover what void God placed you on this Earth to fill. Through these different assessments, you gain clarity of your purpose. You can know which areas in life to focus on and which ones to leave to someone else.

I believe, especially in the early stages of our Christian walk, God gives us little glimpses into what He plans to do with our lives as a whole. When we use this knowledge to His benefit, I believe He expands it and gives us even more room to grown in.

Scripture says in Matthew 25:23 that when we are faithful over a few things, God will make us ruler over many. It's one of my favorite biblical promises. If you don't know what you are starting out with and how to make the most of it, it gets a little hard for God to multiply and expand upon it. So let's step back and assess what things you've already got working.

Divine Design

I was in the fourth grade when I won my first award for writing. I received first place in a poetry contest that was open to grades kindergarten through eighth. Fast forward a few years later and I would be completing a children's book called *The Cloud Factory*, one that never saw the light of day in terms of publishing. Then, jump to 2014 when I became a volunteer in my church's teen ministry. I would eventually teach a group of girls at my first ever girls retreat and was forever changed as I realized the combination of talking to teenage girls and writing was my true calling.

To an innocent bystander, those different pieces may not seem connected. I cannot even say I fully understand all that was at play until I took the time to look back over my life and reflect. Now, because I know how intentional my God is, I can look over all He has been doing since I was ten. I see how His hand was working on the fabric of my life and sewing together all these glimpses of my purpose.

If you have ever had an outfit that was custom-made, you understand the excitement that comes along with picking the fabric and determining the outfit's cut and fit. At some point during the process, you might sit down with a tailor to discuss your personal style and what look you want to achieve with the particular piece they are making. You talk about what colors look best with your skin tone, and have a brief exchange on the versatility of the piece so you know you can wear it again and again. You can hardly wait for the big reveal and you're confident you won't have to fret over whether or not it's right for you because it was a custom-made outfit.

I want you to think of your life as a custom-made outfit and think of God as the tailor who crafted it. During your creation, He sat down with Christ and the Holy Spirit to map out the fabric of your life, its cut and its fit. We know this because in Genesis 1:26, God the Father, Christ the Son and the Holy Spirit said "let us make man in our image, after our likeness."

We have all been handcrafted by God. He picked the color of our eyes, the shape of our feet, the way that we walk, He knew the makeup of our families. There is nothing about us that slipped through the cracks of God's design process and that is why it means so much to Him when we tap into our purpose, when we finally start to connect the dots between all He has been doing.

That is how it was with me. If I looked at each segment of my life individually it was easy to miss something, but once I asked God flat out, what He was doing with me, I started to view the full tapestry and was able to make connections between different things He had been showing me.

You can experience this same type of discovery by paying attention to a few different things. First, figure out your personality. Second, tap into your passion. Third, start using your spiritual gifts (the God-given abilities placed in us when we accepted Jesus Christ as Savior and joined his family). You can think of these as a born again gift. In the next few chapters, we will dive a little deeper into each of these three subjects and find out how they all play a huge part in how we live our life on purpose.

Chapter 1

Lions and Tigers and Bears

You may have started this chapter giving me a slight side eye for the title, but I have a good explanation. At the church I attend, the first lady teaches a class called New Beginnings. The class is eight weeks long and at the end of it we receive a spiritual gifts assessment (we'll talk more about this in Chapter Three. The first lady also has all the new members go through a personality assessment created by David Smalley of the Smalley Institute. [5] There are four different personality types in this test:

- Lions - the leaders of the group
- Beavers - the thinkers who analyze situations before making moves.
- Golden Retrievers - the most loyal of all the personality types.
- Otters - the fun loving people.

I learned that I am primarily otter and golden retriever, with a bit of lion sprinkled in for good measure. My husband, Geordan (pronounced Jordan), is an even split between lion and beaver. This understanding of myself and of him provided a ton of perspective for the both of us, especially when it came to making decisions. He might lean more toward choices based on logic, whereas I might look to the option that is more fun or allows me to spend more time with friends.

G will attest to the fact that if a friend needs to talk, I will stay up all hours of the night listening, no matter how long it takes for them to feel they have reached a sensible and comforting solution. But when Geordan is mentally or physically spent, that is it. Despite what he may want to give, he has already made the decision that he has to get rest in order to be of assistance.

While the animal names may seem silly, the personalities behind them provide a great deal of insight into who God has crafted you to be. You may have a greater appreciation for the kind of job or school that really challenges you to think as a beaver.

If you're an otter, you may be drawn to a place with a lot of activity, and if you're a golden retriever, you may find connections with places that seem to cultivate long-lasting relationships.

My favorite part about taking the personality assessment was recognizing that even the things I found most frustrating about myself were intentional when God created me. Things that at one point may have gotten me in trouble because otters just want to have fun, or left me hurt because I felt my loyalty as a golden retriever wasn't returned were worked into His plan for the life He gave me. No matter how you have used your personality in the past, God can turn it around and use it for His glory. "Therefore, if anyone is in Christ, he is a new creation. The old has passed away; and look, new things have come." (2 Corinthians 5:17, HCSB)

Action Steps

- Take The Smalley Institute's personality assessment online at http://www.smalley.cc/personality-quiz/
- Try and guess the personalities of your friends and then discuss the strengths and weaknesses that each of your personality types possess

Chapter 2

Passion – What Breaks Your Heart?

When my church's Youth and Young Adult ministry started a six-week Bible study series on purpose, my friend and former Youth and Young Adult Pastor, Fred "Chip" Luter III asked all of us, *"What breaks your heart?"* I remember thinking that it was a strange question and I struggled to pinpoint the answer. I also couldn't seem to make the connection between the things that broke my heart and what God put me on this Earth to do.

However, in time, I began to understand the significance of what my pastor was getting at. The thing God allows to break my heart is something He wants me to play a part in solving. For example, one thing that breaks my heart is when young ladies do not seem to understand their value. So instead of God allowing me to sit on the sidelines and be sad about it, He placed this book on my heart and gave me a platform to tell young girls like you, that you have a pre-ordained purpose.

This method of working backwards to solve a problem is not uncommon. Many CEOs and business owners start hashing out their business plan by identifying a problem and then brainstorming solutions. I have an aunt and uncle who started a child-placement agency after working with adults who suffered from drug abuse because they wanted to ensure the children of these individuals didn't repeat the same cycle. My friend Cydni started a brand called "It's Her Strut" after seeing a lack of self-esteem in the women in her community. In addition to providing content that is uplifting, through It's Her Strut, Cydni has been able to host engaging and inspiring events in different cities around the country. I started my own marketing firm in 2014 because I felt too many people in the industry were so focused on money that they missed the opportunity to tell the brand's story and really connect people with what made that particular business unique.

You might see children who don't have a family or people who don't have a home. You may be moved by women who have lost their husbands or men who have lost their jobs. Once you have identified specific needs and prayed to God about how He would have you step in, He will provide you the proper guidance. James 1:5 (NLT) says, "If you need wisdom, ask our generous God and He will give it to you. He will not rebuke you for asking." Even when the problem seems bigger than us, we can be confident knowing that though we don't have it all figured out, we are connected to the One who does.

If you don't know your passion, pray that God will reveal it to you and provide an increased awareness as you move throughout your week. Ask Him to help you pay attention to the areas of your life that cause you emotional distress or pain or to the stories you can't seem to release. Your passion may surprise you, but once you know what it is, life becomes a lot more interesting. Recognizing I was called to help teens gave me great insight into why high school was difficult for me and helped me to realize my experiences would be used to help somebody.

Action Steps

- Make note of the things that "break your heart."
- Brainstorm ideas on how you can help solve issues that excite your passion.
- Pray that God gives you the boldness to implement those ideas

Chapter 3

The ABCs of Spiritual Gifts

There are nine spiritual gifts listed in the Bible: wisdom, knowledge, faith, healing, the ability to perform miracles, prophecy, discernment, speaking in tongues and the interpretation of tongues.

In addition to the nine in the Bible that are explicitly mentioned, many Christian resources and spiritual-gifts tests given today list quite a few more, such as exhortation, evangelism, intercession, giving, serving, teaching, administration, artistry, leadership, writing, mercy, music, shepherding and hospitality. As I said in the introduction, these are considered spiritual gifts instead of talents because no one is born with them, they are received when we are born again. Their primary purpose is for the development of the body of Christ. You will use them in ministry and sometimes, spiritual gifts can shift depending on which ones you spend time developing. Let's take a look at some definitions for each.

Anyone, within the body of Christ, who is well-organized and appreciates when things run efficiently most likely has the spiritual gift of Administration. It is highly likely that this person takes many factors into consideration before moving forward with a plan. If we look to the Bible for an example, we could find one in Luke 14:28-30, in the person who before building a tower, sat down and estimated the cost of building. This person does not jump headfirst into things, they carefully consider their options and then make decisions accordingly.

If you enjoy making things with your hands, your spiritual gift may be Craftsmanship. In Exodus 35, God commanded the Israelites to build a place of worship and the offerings necessary to craft it, show just how immaculate their worship place would be when finished. After the offerings had been made in verse 30 of chapter 35, God chose a man named Bezalel to help build it because the Lord had given him "ability in every kind of craft to design artistic works in gold, silver and bronze to cut gemstones for mounting and to carve wood for work in every kind of artistic craft," (HCSB).

If you realize something bad is about to happen before it happens, you may have the spiritual gift of Discernment or a leading of the Holy Spirit. For example, when I was in college, I got invited to an end-of-the-year party someone was hosting at a place not too far from my apartment. A resounding "no, don't go!" cried out in my head before the person inviting me could even finish their invitation. I didn't understand until the next day when I found out there was a shooting at the party and people were arrested. My gift of discernment shielded me from what turned out to be a terrible event and I know God's hand was all over it. In Psalm 119: 125 David asks God for discernment so that he could understand God's commandments and keep from sinning against Him.

Next, we have Encouragement, Evangelism and Exhortation. Encouragement is the ability to use your words to build people up when they are feeling down. In 1 Thessalonians 5:9-11, we are all directed to encourage one another and build each other up. I find this to be especially important for women.

Evangelism is the ability to share the Gospel with those around you. This does not mean you burst into every room with your Bible flailing in the air, on the contrary, it means that talking about the love of Jesus comes natural because it's personal to you. You talk about Christ with as much ease as you talk about food. People with the gift of evangelism are relational people, whose strong relationships make it easy to share what God has done for them. We see someone with a strong gift for evangelism when we look at Paul. In his letters to the churches in Rome, Corinth and Philippi, Paul spoke in detail about what God had done for him and how believers there should be conducting themselves as members of the faith.

Faith provides the boldness to trust God to fulfill His purpose in your life, it "is the substance of things hoped for and the evidence of things not seen." (Hebrews 11:1, King James). If you have the spiritual gift of faith you may make decisions that no one else can understand but you move forth with confidence that what you are doing is a part of God's plan.

The Bible contains countless examples of men and women who lived lives marked by faith. Many of these are written in what I like to call the Faith Hall of Fame in Hebrews 11. One of my favorite faith stories is about the woman with the issue of blood, who believed, if she could just touch the hem of Jesus' garment she would be healed (Mark 5:25-28) and that's what happened.

Giving is a beautiful spiritual gift that allows you to constantly be on the lookout for the needs of others and cheerfully ask God for ways you can help meet those needs. Giving people are not stingy because they recognize all they have is God's to begin with, and they don't worry about giving more because they understand

God will always provide the proper resources to carry out His work. The widow in Mark 12:41-44 was a great example, scripture says she only gave two small copper coins worth a few cents but it meant the world to Jesus because it was all she had to give. My friend Dudley (the one who designed the book cover) possesses this gift. In one year Dudley received a new house and a new job and I am fully convinced it was a direct result of his willingness to give and a fulfillment of God's promises.

Those with the gift of Hospitality love to open up their homes to their community, whether it's for a social event or to meet a need. They enjoy cooking and meeting new people and are great at making people feel welcomed no matter the setting. Martha, the sister of Mary and Lazarus, possessed this gift. Luke 10 speaks of the way she served Jesus and his disciples when they visited.

The gift of Intercession can be seen as a special ability to pray to meet the needs of those around you. For the person with this gift, praying comes with ease and talking to God for long periods of time is done without tiring. Intercessors often display a great amount of compassion for others. I can't help but think that Paul was also an intercessor. He prayed so passionately for the churches God helped him get started and you could tell he cared deeply for every person within those congregations. His prayers were never surface level, instead they often revolved around spiritual growth for those who needed it. Take, for example, His prayer for the Ephesians: "I pray for you constantly asking God, the glorious Father of our Lord Jesus Christ to give you spiritual wisdom and insight so that you might grow in your knowledge of God. I pray that your hearts will be flooded with light so that you can understand the confident hope he has given to those he called - his holy people who are rich in his glorious inheritance. I also pray that you will understand the incredible greatness of God's power for us who believe in Him." Ephesians 1:16b-19a.

Knowledge is a spiritual gift that ties directly into understanding what the Bible teaches and being able to share that insight with others. People with this gift can make connections between what the Bible says and what is happening in the world today. They spend a great deal of time analyzing the Word of God and gathering additional information. Solomon possessed this gift and used it when he reigned as king after his father David (2 Corinthians 1:7-12).

If you have the spiritual gift of Leadership, you tend to achieve many of your goals. You are able to use your knowledge and personality to inspire your team and drive them towards ministry goals. In Hebrews 13:17 we are told that one day, every leader will have to give an account to Christ for those they led so it is important that we pray for our leaders regularly.

Mercy has a heart for others and their struggles. It conveys love and compassion for those who are enduring tough circumstances. People with the spiritual gift of mercy have deep feelings and may not be able to watch the daily news because reports can become too overwhelming. They are always looking to meet a need of someone around them. Christ showed mercy to the two blind men in Matthew 20:29-34 who begged that he would give them vision. Scripture says all he did was touch their eyes and the blind men were able to see.

Music is a spiritual gift granted by God to move people in an emotional way and heighten the worship experience. People with the spiritual gift of music allows God to use their voices or abilities to play an instrument for His glory. (Psalm 95:1-2). Shepherds are mentors, people blessed with the spiritual gift of leading and guiding those around them to grow in their spiritual walk with God. These people hold great conversations and establish strong relationships with those around them. They tend to nurture those they feel the Lord has put in their care (1 Peter 5:2).

Servants support the work of others with ease and are not concerned with getting credit. In Acts 9, we meet a woman named Tabitha. All scripture says of her is that she was always doing good and helped the poor. Even after she dies and Peter brings her back to life, we don't read anything about her friends or family so it's safe to assume she lived her life behind the scenes.

If you experience joy from helping out around the house or volunteering in your community, it's likely that you have the spiritual gift of Serving. The spiritual gift of Teaching is an ability to convey the meaning of Scripture and communicate it in a way that creates easy understanding and application. Paul is another great example of this gift.

If you have the spiritual gift of Wisdom, you are able to assess a situation from a wider perspective. Time spent in your Bible and praying to God gives you the confidence to make proper decisions and decipher what is real and what isn't. Someone broke it down to me like this: knowledge is what you know and wisdom is what you do with what you know. James 3:13 (HCSB) says "Who is wise and has understanding among you? He should show his works by good conduct with wisdom's gentleness."

Writing is the ability to express wisdom, knowledge and understanding in a form that can be read by others.

If you have this gift, it is likely that you have written a note of encouragement, a poem, song, story or sermon that has strongly impacted the life of someone else. Words come forth naturally and may even be a part of helping you process something you have felt from the Holy Spirit. Journaling may be one of your hobbies and you may find that you experience increased clarity after you've taken the time to write down what you're thinking.

As you can see, the body of Christ is extremely diverse in terms of the gifts we all receive. God uses all of these for the expansion of His Kingdom and equips us to be able to go out into the world and reach others who are drawn to us because of our ministry.

God may place you at a church that is struggling with their music ministry so you can make a contribution. He may have put you in a place where you can show hospitality to others by starting a weekly Bible study meeting at your house or you may be in a neighborhood that could benefit from some acts of service, such as picking up trash or cutting grass. God sees and can use you in all of these instances.

When and only if you accept Christ, I encourage you to take a spiritual gifts assessment. There are a number of spiritual gifts tests online. My favorite is spiritualgiftstest.com because it's easy to navigate.

You can complete it to find out what your spiritual gifts may be. I guarantee that when you determine your calling, the process of discovering how God will use them is inspiring.

Action Steps

- Take a spiritual gifts test online at spiritualgiftstest.com
- Encourage one of your friends to take it with you and discuss your similarities and differences.
- Talk to someone at your church about the results and ask what ministries might benefit most from your spiritual gifts.

Part 2:

Positioned for your Purpose

"For God knew his people in advance, and He chose them to become like His son, so that His son would be the firstborn among many brothers and sisters."
Romans 8:29 (HCSB)

I once heard a story about two farmers who were praying for rain. One farmer kept praying and praying as the other one started to prepare a place as if the rain has already come. If you want to walk in the will of God, it's crucial that you position yourself to hear from Him. This means putting forth a constant effort to become more like His son who died for our sins. In the following chapters we are going to look at five major areas of life, that once aligned with God, can change everything. It's all a matter of positioning.

Spiritual Life

It would be impossible and irresponsible for me to start this positioning section with anything outside of spirituality. Largely because if you are not connected to God the Father, Christ the Son, and the Holy Spirit spiritually then this book becomes irrelevant and loses its greater meaning.

Some people interpret spirituality as a deep understanding of their inner "being." If you are a born again believer that "being" is Christ in the form of the Holy Spirit and an understanding of all He is and has to offer has a domino affect on everything.

Emotions can and do change with the wind, our job titles will vary from year to year, our physical appearance can be easily altered through working out and dieting and our recreational activities will likely change based on where we live, our age and the people we spend our down time with. If we want to have a solid foundation, Christ must be at the center of it.

Chapter 4

What Do I Believe?

Have you ever stopped to ask yourself that question? It's a pretty heavy one and requires complete honesty, especially if you are dedicated to living purposefully.

I remember the day I realized I wasn't really firm in what I believed. I knew Jesus was Lord, that he died on this cross for my sins so I could live eternally but I wasn't confident in my salvation and sometimes doubted that if Christ came back, he would be coming for me.

If you're reading this book, you might be someone like me. You were born and raised in the church, you may have received your education at a Christian school, had to choose between being a youth usher or being the choir and now as you look over all the childhood memories that revolved around the church you're not sure if those experiences taught you anything. You're not sure if, even after all that time in church, you know what you believe.

Maybe you have never encountered Christ or entered the walls of a church. You just happened to come across this book and found the title to be intriguing. For some authors, this would be the part of the book where you are condemned to hell and told to get your life right today because Judgment Day is coming. The latter part would be true, Judgment Day is coming (see Revelations) but I believe God wants you to have a relationship with Him that's built on a love foundation, not fear of condemnation. I have never been a fan of people who try to scare someone into faith in Jesus Christ because I believe love lasts longer than intimidation. Painting God as this big bully in the sky who forces you to be with Him is largely inaccurate because as we discussed in the opening God made man in His image.

God's intention has always been to live in fellowship with man but since Adam and Even broke that fellowship (see Genesis) the story of God and His love for us has been one of reconciliation. It is with this background context in mind that I tell you no matter if at present you believe, I am confident God is the one who placed this book in your hands and belief in Him will change your life.

For years, I rode on the coattails of my parents' faith but had not truly pursued a personal relationship with Jesus Christ, in whom I said I believed. I found the realization to be alarming and doubt started to creep in as I wondered if I was as saved or if I was just pretending. That question sparked something inside of me and I spent six months really digging into what it meant to be a Christian. Looking back at that period of my life, I thank God for my awakening because it allowed me to build up my knowledge and confidence. Today I have no doubt in my mind that when I leave this Earth, it will be to spend eternity in heaven.

Today, I enjoy the benefits of getting to know more about Christ through reading the Bible, worshipping and spending time collectively in group Bible studies and individually, in prayer. I can't help but be wowed by all he has done and continues to do for me. The more I discover the more impossible it seems for me not to return the love of Jesus Christ, because he loved me so deeply he died for me and that love continues to change me. It has inspired me to not just be a Christian or Christ-follower in title but to be one in deed.

Christ says "By this all men will know that you are my disciples, if you have love for one another" John 13:35 (NASB) and James 2:24 (CEV) says "We please God by what we do and not only by what we believe." This means our relationship with Christ should be visible to everyone we meet. They should see it in the way we walk, the way we talk, the kind of things we allow ourselves to watch on TV. It should be evident in the way we live and the way we give, and through the contributions we make to our community. You may be thinking that sounds hard but once you have turned your life over to Christ, He will start changing you piece by piece. You will not have to "get ready" for salvation, you just have to join in on God's family. He takes all the brokenness, the shame and the guilt and little by little starts to peel off the filth of your past. What's better is, He doesn't bring it up again.

I remember wearing all white the day I was baptized by choice for the second time. I could almost hear Christ whisper, *"you're forgiven"* as I stared at the mirror in from of me. He wasn't shaming me for trying to put Him in a box my first couple years of college or only talking to Him when I needed something, He was happy that I had returned and was ready to be used for His purpose.

You may believe, based on your particular experience, that following Christ is this big book of things you can't do, but I am here to tell you there is far more to it. As your love for Christ grows, so will your appetite to do the things that please him. All the things I thought I would be "missing out on" in life pale in comparison to what I have gained through Him. A holy encounter took place between myself and the Holy Spirit. I knew I would never be the same person I was before I met Him.

Before Christ died for man, we were all slaves to sin and and time in the Bible tells us sin is a dead end. "For the wages of sin is death, but the gift of God is eternal life in Christ Jesus our Lord." (Romans 6:23, HCSB) When we commit to Christ and surrender our sinful nature over to him, purpose-driven living can begin. It stops being about where we were before Christ and shifts to where we are going with Him.

All it takes to get plugged in is admission, confession and belief. We find this in Romans 10:9 (NASB) "that if you confess with your mouth Jesus is Lord, and believe in your heart that God has raised him from the dead, you will be saved."

The enemy would love nothing more than you to doubt what I'm saying because he knows what I know - belief in Christ is the start to a life you won't believe. John 10:10 says, "the thief [Satan] comes only to steal, kill and destroy. I came so that they might have life and have it in abundance." If you are ready for abundant living, "The Spirit and the Bride say, 'Come!' Everyone who hears this must also say, 'Come!' Come, whoever is thirsty; accept the water of life as a gift, whoever wants it." (Romans 22:17, GNT)

Action Steps

- If you want to know more about Christ so you can stand firmly on what you believe, spend some time in the Gospels of Matthew, Mark, Luke and John.

- If you have studied for yourself, but are still having a hard time getting into this "follower of Christ" thing, read the book of James. James was Jesus' half-brother and was one of his biggest critics, but it took one encounter after Christ was raised from the dead for James to become a proclaimer of the Gospel.

- If you are ready to accept Jesus Christ as your Savior, follow the ABCs to salvation:

  - Admit that you are a sinner and want to turn away from your sins (Romans 3:23, Romans 6:23, 1 John 1:9)

  - Believe that Jesus Christ died on the cross for your sins and rose again on the third day (John 3:16, Romans 5:8)

  - Confess that Jesus is now Lord over your life (Romans 10:9)

Chapter 5

The Importance of Prayer

If you grew up in the church, I'm sure you are familiar with the model prayer - "Our Father, who art in heaven. Hallowed be thy name. Thy Kingdom come, thy will be done on Earth as it is in heaven..." (Matthew 6:9-10). I found the model prayer to be extremely intimidating when I was younger.

Can you blame me? It uses words like "hallowed." When I sat down and thought about it, I couldn't help but notice that the reverence and respect surrounding the Lord's Prayer made my spiritual life feel like an awkward first date. I would start out knowing all the words I wanted to say, but the moment I opened my mouth, my mind would go blank.

Only when I started to view prayer as a conversation with God did I become more comfortable praying. I stopped believing I had to have topics ready and opened myself up to simply letting my words flow naturally. If you have no prior experience with prayer, The Model Prayer is a good place to get started, especially if you read it in a translation that's easy for you to understand. Notice there are four main parts that Christ mentions: praying in community, expressing adoration, asking God for what we need and confessing our sin to Him. Let's read the prayer in its entirety:

"Therefore, you should pray like this: Our Father in heaven, Your name be honored as holy. Your Kingdom come. Your will be done on earth as it is in heaven. Give us today our daily bread. And forgive us our debts, as we also have forgiven our debtors. And do not bring us into temptation, but deliver us from the evil one. For Yours is the Kingdom and the power and the glory forever. Amen." (Matthew 6:9-13, HCSB)

Praying in Community

One Sunday when visiting a friend's church, I was introduced to a part of the prayer I never fully grasped. As Jesus teaches the new believers about prayer, he starts the model off with three important letters o-u-r. "Our Father," not "my Father." So it's safe to assume Christ believed anyone who was praying this prayer would be praying within a community of fellow believers.

Why might this be? For an answer we can look to Matthew 18:19 (HCSB) - "Again, I assure you: If two of you on earth agree about any matter that you pray for, it will be done for you by My Father in heaven."

Promises don't get much clearer. Christ says when we pray in community and agree, then we can be confident we will receive that for which we have asked as long as it aligns with God's will. Another benefit of praying in community is that as we are transparent about our needs with the people God has placed in our lives and are comfortable enough to share those needs openly in prayer we establish room for a testimony. We create a safe space for other newcomers to share what they're struggling with and demonstrate faith that God hears our prayers and responds to them as He deems necessary.

Expressing Adoration

Once Jesus stresses the importance of praying together by his simple use of the word "our," we see he continues his prayer to God with adoration. Jesus recognizes God's character and praises Him for who He is. He says, "Let your name be honored as holy (v. 9). When we take a moment in our prayer to adore our Lord God, we are able to gain the proper perspective of the one to Whom we are speaking.

Sometimes in the midst of a hard situation, I can forget that God is big, powerful, sovereign and interested in what I have to say to Him. I can get so bogged down by my current circumstances that I convince myself that He may not want to hear about my problems or that I would be better off trying to solve them on my own.

I am able to avoid this temptation when I share how much I adore Him. There is something marvelous about reflecting on His greatness and it always brings me back to a place of confidence where I know there is nothing impossible for Him (Genesis 18:9-15, John 11:17-44, Luke 24:1-6).

Confessing Our Sin

After expressing adoration, Jesus teaches that we are to confess our sins and ask for forgiveness. He actually does this after petitioning God for our needs but I like talking to God with a clean slate. As I have matured in my faith I will confess my sin almost immediately because it does not take the Holy Spirit long to convict me. But there are still sins I may commit without even thinking.

In verse 12, Christ says, "forgive us our debts as we have also forgiven our debtors." We ask God to forgive our sins and to help us to forgive those who have sinned against us - more about this to come in Chapter Nine.

Confession of sin, maintains the health of our relationship with Christ. Denial of sin puts our fellowship with Him at risk. We by no means, lose our salvation, but it can be a lot harder to hear from Him when He is speaking or when we are asking Him for direction.

King David experienced this firsthand after not confessing to God that he had slept with another man's wife, gotten her pregnant and then had her husband killed (2 Samuel 11). In Psalm 32:3b (NLT), David says, "Day and night [God's] hand of discipline was heavy on me. My strength had evaporated like water in the summer heat."

The king paints a vivid picture of how it feels to be out of fellowship with God, but if we continue reading, we see he was ready to repent. Psalm 32:5 (NLT) says, "Finally, I confessed all my sins to you and stopped trying to hide my guilt. I said to myself 'I will confess my rebellion to the Lord and you forgave me. All my guilt is gone.'" There is no sin we have committed that God does not already know about but we still must confess it and seek reconciliation.

Our prayer time provides us with the perfect opportunity to confess it. When we do this, we can share in David's experience: freedom of guilt and the chance to live a life God is pleased with.

Asking God for What You Need

We see in the model prayer that Christ encourages us to ask God for what we need. This is called supplication. In Matthew 6:10, Jesus says, "Give us today our daily bread" and in verse 13, he says, "lead us not into temptation but deliver us from the evil one." These verses cover two major needs: physical: food, shelter, clothing and spiritual: the strength to overcome temptations that may come our way.

I have found that asking God for what I need reminds me that I cannot get whatever it is on my own, it also fosters a heart of thanksgiving when I find out that God heard my need and supplied according to His riches in glory (Philippians 4:19).

In addition to our own needs, supplication allows us to petition God on behalf of others. Sometimes, I kneel down to pray for myself or my immediate family and God will put someone else on my heart. Before I know it, I have spent more time praying for their needs than my own. This is never a bad thing, because as we pray for others and empathize with them, we are following a specific directive. James 5:16a (HCSB) says, "Therefore, confess your sins to one another and pray for one another, so that you may be healed." You never know, as you're praying for someone else, someone else could be praying for you.

In review, the main parts of the model prayer are praying in community, expressing adoration for God's character, asking for forgiveness of sin and petitioning God to meet our needs. Ultimately, prayer is a conversation and just like any conversation we would have with a friend, it is my belief that God wants our talks with Him to be genuine, not mere repetition. You will find that as you talk to God regularly, it will become easier to submit yourself to His will and open yourself up to the possibilities of what He will do through your purpose-driven living.

Action Steps

- Spend some time reviewing the model prayer in Matthew 6:9-13.
- Set an alarm to help make prayer a part of your daily routine.
- Start keeping a journal of things you have prayed for and mark when your prayers have been answered.

Chapter 6

Quiet Time and Sabbath

If you were to search the web about the Sabbath, you would be sure to find a number of articles arguing both for and against keeping it as tradition. One side of the argument cites the Sabbath as a ritual that must be kept as it was in the time of the Israelites - no work, no chores, no purchases, no baking and, if you pay attention to Scripture, not leaving your house. The other side of the argument goes with a more laid back view of the Sabbath and simply suggests taking time out, whether it be a whole day or a long afternoon, to just rest and process everything you have endured throughout the week.

Truth be told the Sabbath is a tricky thing for me. I have been on both sides of the fence. I have even had weeks when I ignored the Sabbath completely. Those weeks did not go well for me. Geordan and I practiced it in the traditional sense for a few months and I found it to be extremely difficult. A huge reason being that I had friends and family with busy schedules during the week who would rely on Saturdays to be our time for hanging out together. Saturdays, being the seventh day of the week, were supposed to be the days set aside to refrain from activity. This reflects the way God rested on the seventh day during the Creation to reflect on all He had made (Genesis 2:3).

Because one of my love languages[6] is quality time, not doing much with my friends or family on Saturday made me feel isolated and restless. I felt a need to plug in with those around me. This led to implementation of chill activities like going to the park or taking a walk around the neighborhood, I even spent one Sabbath day at the beach with my roommates. I would always bring my Bible and other Bible study resources to remind me that I was able to enjoy my day because of God and I wanted to recommit myself to Him continuously.

At the time of this book's publication I have learned that avoiding rest and even running away from quiet time with God by replacing him with my friends does not serve me. So, I do my best to rest regularly and not avoid quality time with the One who gives me all I need.

As someone who has a checklist for everything, making a conscious decision to spend at least one day a week going with the flow, relaxing and talking to God at a more relaxed pace is a huge test for me. But by the power of the Holy Spirit, and by following Geordan's lead, I have seen that every moment of every day does not have to be filled doing something. Sometimes it's in those quiet moments when I will hear from God most clearly. This provides me with all the motivation I need to make sure I am checking in with Him regularly.

When executed properly, the Sabbath and carved out quiet time keep our lives from being one long run-on sentence by allowing us to put a period at the end of our week. This allows us to gain some perspective on our surroundings and think over what we have achieved that week and what we could have done differently. It creates a clean break from previous days and allows us to start each week with a renewed sense of energy.

In the story of creation, God sat back at the end of each day and admired what He had done saying "It is good" and at the end of the first six days of putting the stars, the waters, animals and humans into place, God took an entire day to look upon all He made and He declared it to be good. I think one of the biggest pitfalls of our society and even our generation is that we are always looking to the next thing. We never allow the weight of being done with huge projects or finishing a grade or excelling at work all week truly set in and so we jump from task to task creating the illusion that we have not accomplished much of anything.

Never taking a break and always having a task pinned to our to-do lists makes life overwhelming. But, when we break our to-dos into bite-sized pieces, prioritizing and knocking things out effectively, we can rest peacefully. Setting aside a specific day to rest also discourages procrastinating because by giving yourself "fewer days" to work with, you will have to work more efficiently. This takes place through the process of prioritizing.

One of the best gifts I've ever received, was an email from a fellow ministry leader that contained a template called The Daily Docket.[7] This beautiful tool allows you to place the three most important items you need to accomplish for your day in an itemized list. I can't tell you how much better it feels to do three things well instead of only half-way doing ten.

It gives the work day an expected end and provides permission to truly rest when the day is finished. When I first started using The Daily Docket, I had to fight the temptation to not do more than the three items. This didn't mean if I finished everything early in the day, I would sit on my hands until it was time to go to sleep. Instead, it allowed me to work on additional things at a more relaxed pace because I understood anything beyond my three most important tasks were just the cherries on top of my day.

If you don't really see yourself as a checklist person that is completely fine, but you must find a way to work effectively so rest is a part of your daily routine. Note I'm not just talking about sleeping. I mean setting a time and space to free your mind of all the world's weight.

When you find yourself continuing to repeat the same "to-dos" in your head again and again, you may benefit from putting them on paper and out of your head. My dad has always been a huge fan and practitioner of this concept. It's highly likely that I get my love of scratching things off a checklist from all my time as a kid running errands with him.

I believe if you implement Sabbath rest and quiet time into your week, you will find yourself mentally equipped to seek God and reflect on where He has brought you thus far. You can journal to clear your mind of all noisy thoughts or you can just stare at the ceiling. I have found this practice to be a lot easier when I put my phone on airplane mode, if at no other time than right before I go to sleep. I do not turn airplane mode off until at least two hours after I wake up the next morning.

This gives me the space to think clearly and focus in on resetting from the constant demands that I experience throughout the day. It also allows me to ease into my day instead of jumping headfirst into emails, texts and social media notifications demanding my attention.

In the Bible, we see how Christ would go somewhere to be alone with God before and after a long day of activity (Matthew 14:23, Luke 6:12, Luke 22:41-44). Now, if Christ, a member of the Trinity and the One who died to save you and me, set aside time for Sabbath moments, how can we think it's something we don't need?

Action Steps

- Try putting your phone on airplane mode this evening before you go to sleep and fight the urge to look at it first thing in the morning.
- Spend some time using the Daily Docket, available at theartofsimple.net for a week and journal about any changes you see in your productivity.
- Read Luke 5 and pay special attention to verses 15-16. Jesus was a busy man but he still had his priorities straight.

Chapter 7

Worship – What Does It Look Like to Me?

I almost didn't include a chapter on worship. It just seemed like such an ambiguous and lofty topic; but I couldn't deny the importance of living a life filled with worship. I could not deny the truth that the way we worship God greatly impacts all the other areas of our lives on a daily basis. How I experience worship and how others experience worship are different.

Even the Bible is loose in its interpretation but I can confidently say contrary to popular belief worship is a great deal more than clapping your hands and swaying during church service. The scripture that best includes all that worship is can be found in Romans 12:1 (HCSB), it reads "Therefore, brothers, by the mercies of God, I urge you to present your bodies as a living sacrifice, holy and pleasing to God; this is your spiritual worship."

Time

Have you ever felt the urge to just sit still? Like a voice inside your head was prompting you to just enjoy some quiet time and stop moving? I once had my friend Lila write about her worship experience and she called these moments "worshipping in silence." Lila said sometimes it is impossible to experience true worship without silence and one day heard God say, "*How do you expect to hear from Me if you are constantly surrounded by noise?*"

The Bible tells us that God's voice is still and soft (1 Kings 19:11-12). This means He is not going to yell over our TVs or radios or turn up His volume because our phone rings. We have to actively seek Him by going to a quiet place and being still before Him. Psalm 46:10ᵃ says, "Be still and know that I am God." That simple act, known as meditation, can be the start to your worship experience.

Meditation is a great way to welcome the Holy Spirit because it's your way of saying "God no matter what is going on around me right now, I am going to focus on you and what your Word says." I feel like King David would share this sentiment. The Bible shows us when

David felt overwhelmed by daily struggles and was experiencing hardships, he often meditated. He even references meditation seven times in Psalm 119 alone. In verse 15 (HCSB), he says, "I will meditate on your precepts and think about your ways" and in verse 27, "Help me understand the meaning of your precepts so that I can understand your wonders."

David makes a direct connection between meditation and understanding. Through meditation we gain clarity, become renewed spiritually and obtain a more intimate relationship with our Father in heaven. Just take a moment to think about what God has done in your life, and remember how He kept you during times of affliction. That time of reflection can lead to an intense and intentional period of worship.

Money

I remember being at a pharmacy one night and a man approached me and asked if I had any money I could give. He was trying to get enough to pay his entrance into the homeless shelter down the street. I emptied my wallet of the few quarters, nickels and dimes I had and then went into the store figuring I had given something so God was pleased with me. I was wrong.

As I prepared to leave the pharmacy, I felt the Holy Spirit prompt me to ask the man the full amount he would need to pay the entrance fee into the shelter down the street. I felt like God was asking a lot of me, what if the amount was more than I had on me? But God assured He would supply all my needs and the scripture Proverbs 19:17 (NLT) came rushing to me "If you help the poor, you are lending to the Lord and he will repay you."

I had to believe that if God was prompting me to give this man some money, then He already had a plan for how He would sustain me until my next paycheck and of course, He did.

Energy

Now this has been a huge area of growth for me. Those who are close to me will tell you I have a high level of sensitivity. For whatever reason, I can take offense to anything easily and this zaps my energy. Instead of being productive for God and letting Him use me, I end up spending more time focusing on someone or something that I have allowed to "make" me unhappy.

What's funny is the moment I decide to let go of whatever I'm dealing with, I feel an instant sense of peace. One day, someone hurt my feelings and I cried out to God asking that He would help me to get over the situation and guide my energy back to His purposes. His response was nearly instant as one of my favorite worship songs played from my playlist, "So in Love" by Jason Nelson. In the chorus Nelson says "nothing will ever distract me from loving You." Oh how I long for that to be true every day of my life, because in the moments it's not, I have just chosen to give my energy to something outside of God. I have redirected my worship.

We must make a conscious effort to call out to God in the moments when we feel our hearts pulling away from Him. The first of the ten commandments says we should have no other gods before God (Exodus 20:3). This could be our families, friendships, finances, relationship, or our job. It can be anything that has taken God's place on the throne of our heart.

When you find yourselves making excuses as to why you can't go to church or read your Bible, you might want to check in and see if your worship needs some redirecting. Sometimes, I can watch a TV show as a way to relax and end up more drained than when I started, but when I use my energy to tap into God's resources I always walk away feeling rejuvenated.

One of the purest worship experiences I ever had, took place while I was waiting for my sister to come out of an emergency room on Christmas night. Instead of worrying, I decided to worship. As I sat reflecting on all God had done, I could not help but trust that He would come through this time too and as I thought of all the people who were spending their night in the hospital, I realized any one of them could have been me or a member of my family. Instead, God sent Brittany out with a routine prescription and I got to spend the rest of my evening in worship.

Action Steps

- Be honest with yourself about the things that may have replaced God on the throne of your heart
- Think through ways you can worship God through your time, money and energy today
- Allow God to reveal what things in your life may be preventing you from worshipping.

Chapter 8

What Does It Mean to Be a Disciple?

In Matthew 28:19-20 (HCSB), believers are given what's often referred to as "The Great Commission." In it, Jesus says "Go therefore and make disciples of all nations, baptizing them in the name of the Father and of the Son and of the Holy Spirit, teaching them to observe everything I have commanded you and remember I am with you always, to the end of the age."

Notice, he gives no further definition into what a disciple is, there is an understanding that these eleven men understood the concept because they lived it for as long as they had been following him.

If we as Christ's disciples are to make disciples, it's critical that we also know what one is. The textbook definition is a follower and many dictionaries define it as one of the 12 men who followed Christ. This is a helpful definition given that these twelve men, outside of Judas

in the end (Luke 22:3-5, Matthew 27:3-5), en
it meant to give up the lives they had planned
themselves for the sake of living out Christ's mission to
share the Gospel and the story of redemption.

Today's society seems far more concerned with
getting to the front and leading everyone else than they
are with following. But as Christians, we must surrender
to the reality that if we're living for Christ, he has to be
the leader, not us. The disciples understood this concept.
Time spent in our Bible shows us these men did much
more than follow Jesus from one place to the next.
During his three years of ministry, these these disciples,
these "followers" studied the word with Christ,
fellowshipped with Him, through the power of the Holy
Spirit were able to perform miracles like Jesus did, they
prayed with him and worshipped with him.

It is safe to assume the disciples had to leave jobs,
family and friends for Christ's sake but when the time
came for Christ's crucifixion, they were and forever will be
associated with him because they were the ones he left
behind to share the Gospel wherever they went. It is
because of these men that you and I are even able to
know who Jesus is. Let that fact sink in. If these twelve
men had kept the good news to themselves, you and I
would never have gotten the chance to be born again.

It is with that recognition that we should be willing to give our lives up for Christ, the way they did. We should walk like Christ, talk like Christ, we should love like him, we should avoid giving into sinful desires that would hurt his reputation or make Christians appear to be hypocrites and be willing to give up the life we had before knowing him (Luke 9:23-24). We should be bold enough to share the Gospel with whoever we meet or "evangelizing.".

I used to freak out at the site of any word with "evangelize" in it. I couldn't help but think I'd have to go from door to door asking if people if they knew the Lord. Over time with an increased study of God's word I realized that He did not expect me to do any brow beating. I simply had to stay armed with His Word and respond to His Holy Spirit's leading.

Anytime we look to our own strength to share the Gospel, it's easy to miss something. But if we pray that God will guide our encounters and our speech, we can be confident that He will get the glory from every interaction we have with those new to the faith or who have never even been exposed to the Gospel. We will be able to peacefully deal with people who may persecute us for sharing our faith.

The disciples had to endure this kind of threat on a daily basis and Jesus knew this. So before he was crucified, he provided some words of encouragement, "Whenever they bring you before synagogues and rulers and authorities, don't worry about how you should defend yourselves or what you should say. For the Holy Spirit will teach you at that very hour what must be said." (Luke 12:11-12, HCSB)

God does not call us to do anything without simultaneously providing the tools necessary for us to succeed. When it comes to sharing the Gospel, once you have planted the first seed into someone's heart, it's easier to keep watering. This may be through studying the Word with believers who are new in the faith or helping those who don't know how to pray by breaking down the model prayer the way we did in Chapter Five. There are tons of possibilities.

Action Steps

- Look for opportunities to help build up fellow believers and witness to nonbelievers.
- Try to establish a Paul, Barnabas and Timothy model - someone you can look to for spiritual advice, someone on your level and someone to disciple.
- Start or join a small group so talking about your faith can become more natural

Emotional Life

If you grew up with brothers, male cousins or even if you have male friends, at some point you've likely been characterized by one of them as being "emotional" or "overly sensitive." When I hear those words, I have to fight the urge to be defensive because I feel they tend to dismiss any logic I possess, no matter the situation.

I'm blessed enough to have a dad who always allows me to talk through my feelings and because I've been given that freedom, over time, I have grown to be less defensive. I have come to realize that we (men and women alike) were designed to embrace our emotions.

We are emotional because God is emotional and He made us in His image. As humans we experience a wide range of emotions including joy, sadness, love and peacefulness. I find that many times these emotions can draw us closer to God but when emotions drive us away from Him, they keep us from purpose-driven living. In this section of the book, I plan to highlight a few of those emotions and discuss how we can combat them.

Chapter 9

Thoughts that Give Life: Winning the Battle Over Anger, the Inability to Forgive, Worry and Thoughts of Suicide

In the Bible, we see numerous occasions when Jesus Christ did not shy away from showing his emotion. He had periods of anger (Mark 3:1-6, Mark 11:5). He had periods of sadness like when his friend Lazarus died in John 11:35 and he experienced most other conceivable emotions. What set him apart though is that we don't see anywhere in scripture where Christ was unforgiving.

You can't find a place in the Bible that talks about him being crippled with worry and he doesn't cut his life short before fulfilling his calling. That's why Hebrews 4:15 (HCSB) boldly says, "For we do not have a high priest who is unable to sympathize with our weaknesses, but One who has been tested in every way as we are, yet without sin." Let's observe these emotions separately and see how Christ would deal with them.

Anger

As I sat on the passenger side of his car, screaming at him and beating my hands against the dashboard, a quiet voice said, *"You are causing damage to your relationship."* But my shouts were louder than the small voice in my head, so I continued my anger fit, oblivious to its long-term effects. I wanted to be heard and if that meant I needed to scream, then Geordan would just have to deal with it.

Years later, I have developed a better method of communicating. I try with all my might to seek to understand before I try to be understood. I have also learned through many years of being with Geordan that just because I raise my voice, does not mean he is more likely to hear me. Often the harsh tone I might be using offends him and that does not give God glory.

Another side of anger that does not give God glory is the kind of anger that is held within. Contrary to the kind of anger that's loud and belligerent, this breed of anger feeds off itself and feeds off thoughts of revenge.

No matter what qualification of anger you identify with, both can be silent killers. Like the serpent in the Garden of Eden (Genesis 3:1) anger in any form can be cunning and its outbursts are hard to measure. It may start out with yelling at another driver or rolling our eyes when someone says something annoying. Then it escalates to verbal altercations with teachers and fellow classmates, some even using foul language. We tell ourselves we're not angry, we're just "passionate."

Well love, I have to tell you something: you and I and all of humanity have an anger problem that began those thousands of years ago in that same garden. Hope lies in the fact that anger in and of itself is not a sin. We see that Christ was angry many times in the Bible, like in John 2:15-17. Often it's how we choose to deal with our anger that causes issues.

Ephesians 4:26 (HCSB) says, "Be angry and do not sin. Do not let the sun go down on your anger." In order to follow that command, we must start trying to figure out the root of our anger so we can properly deal with it. I realized anger was often the way I showed Geordan I was hurt by his words or actions. It took a long time for me to be able to understand my behavior and find a better way to express my discontent, but when I finally did, our relationship was strengthened. I started taking responsibility for emotions and took much of the pressure off of him. Sometimes we allow our anger to keep brewing, but if we make up our minds that we are going to let go of negative feelings, we create space to function appropriately and move on to more pleasant things.

"Man's anger does not accomplish God's righteousness," James 1:20 (HCSB), so the moment we let go of our harsh emotions, we allow God to come in and heal us where we need it. What's more, our godly reactions can be a witness to whoever we are holding a conversation with.

Sometimes I have to stop mid-sentence and pray while I am talking to someone because I have found it is nearly impossible to be mad at them while praying for them. I know this practice can help you too, and when properly implemented will help you avoid screaming at your boyfriend, your best friend or anyone else from the passenger side of a car. Instead, you'll be able to conduct yourself in a loving fashion.

Forgiveness

I am the oldest grandchild on both sides of my family and as I watch my younger sister, Brittany and all my cousins grow up, I find myself occasionally reflecting on how all of us used to be. Needless to say, we didn't always display the most maturity. If one of us did something to the other, we would usually start fussing and our parents would make someone say that they were sorry.

I remember how much it would pain me to say those words, even if I knew I was guilty, but oh, how I enjoyed being the one who was accepting the apology. Even if I said I forgave them, that forgiveness rarely took place immediately. I am so glad that is not the way God forgives you and me.

The Bible tells us that when we confess, God not only forgives our sins, but He forgets them. "I – yes, I alone - will blot out your sins for my own sake and never think of them again." (Isaiah 43:25, NLT). We see this when we look at Christ. He is the only one who was able to walk this Earth as a man and not sin. It's hard to compare ourselves to him, but the Bible provides us with the story of an ordinary man who came close to forgiving the way Christ does. His name was Joseph.

Joseph was the youngest of 11 boys (his brother Benjamin came along later) and Joseph's father Jacob made it obvious to everyone that Joseph was his favorite son. One day, all of Joseph's brothers got tired of dad's favorite so they sold Joseph into slavery and let their father think he was dead.

God allowed Joseph to be sold to a fair man named Potiphar. Everything was going along smoothly until Potiphar's wife developed a crush on Joseph. One night, when he refused to sleep with her, Potiphar's wife accused Joseph of rape and he was thrown in jail. Joseph was only released from jail after a series of events over the course of several years that included dream interpretation. Joseph interprets one of Pharaoh's dreams and is promoted to second in rank to Pharaoh. Later, Joseph comes up with a plan to sustain everyone when a famine hits the land.

That plan brought Joseph face-to-face with his brothers who needed some of the food his country had stored away. They did not recognize him. In their minds Joseph was dead. This put Joseph in a very powerful position. He could have made his brothers pay for selling him into slavery. One word from him and his brothers could have been sentenced to death or locked up in prison, but, as much as it hurt him, Joseph chose to forgive because he could see God's hand in everything that happened.

Even when his brothers were willing to become slaves to him, Joseph told them, "Don't be afraid of me. Am I God, that I can punish you? You intended to harm me, but God intended it all for good. He brought me to this position so I could save the lives of many people." (Genesis 50:19-20, NLT)

There may be someone in your life who has hurt you deeply, and for days, weeks, months or even years, you have been holding onto resentment. But no matter what the hurt, it is time to let go and forgive, just like Joseph. Matthew 6:14 (HCSB) says, "For if you forgive people their wrongdoing, your heavenly Father will forgive you as well." When we practice forgiveness, we maintain a healthy relationship with Christ and ensure we are always in a place to receive God's forgiveness. We are able to display our maturity in Christ and forgive like he forgives.

Worry

As I looked through my front window at the red truck that was pressed up against the rear of my car, I thought to myself "that's odd." The Brie from a year before would have screamed or cried out "My car! Why me?" but who I was in that moment simply took in the scene and said to God, "I guess you decided you wanted this to be a part of my day."

I stepped outside in peace only to be greeted by the men who had caused the four-car collision. "You know who car this for?" I politely told them though I did not know the owner of the red truck, the white car that had been hit was mine. They were speechless.

I spent most of that afternoon sitting on the front porch waiting for the police to arrive and write a report. I purposefully avoided the urge to relay the situation in my head. I didn't start thinking about how I would find the money to get my car fixed. I just sat on my porch and read knowing my peace came from recognizing how silly it is for me to worry.

Luke 12:25 (NLT) says "Can all your worries add a single moment to your life?" Meditation on that scripture alone led me to reevaluate what worrying did to and for me. I knew the answer to the scripture's poignant question was "no." Worry could not add a single moment to my life but it could steal moments from me.

That's when I decided to do something crazy. I committed myself to trust God with everything. Whether it be time, money, friends or family, I began to understand that all I have is His and what He has given, He can also take away in a moment's notice. This realization made me feel free. I am at a point now where I can't count the number of planes I've almost missed, or the number of unexpected bills I have gotten in the mail that sparked little to no reaction.

I have just started to think to myself, as I did when my car was hit, "I guess this is something God wanted to be a part of my day" and rolled with it. There is no peace like the peace God provides in those moments, but we only get to that place when we keep our minds on Him. Philippians 4:6 (NLT) says, "Don't worry about anything; instead, pray about everything. Tell God what you need, and thank him for all he has done."

When you have a test coming up, talk to God about it. Tell Him your concerns and then trust that He will bring you through it. When you have more month left then money, if needed, confess any sin that got you to that place and then pray that God will sustain you until your next check or allowance. If a family member is sick, tell God how you feel affected and then make up in your mind that you will continue to put your faith in Him.

Hebrews 11:6 (HCSB) says "Now without faith it is impossible to please God, for the one who draws near to Him must believe He exists and rewards those who seek Him." It is silly to lay down your burdens before God if you have no intention to leave them. When you see the way He takes care of your every need and is there for you in every situation, it becomes easier to trust His heart even when you can't understand His plan.

I know worrying isn't something you can stop doing overnight. It's a gradual process, so for now start with worrying less. One day you look up and find yourself strengthened to deal with whatever comes your way.

You may even be able to provide encouragement to someone around you who seems to constantly be worrying. Your life can be a living testimony to the peace God provides that surpasses all understanding. (Philippians 4:7)

Suicide

"This is not the end of your story," my mom said as I sat on the edge of my bed. "God has something great planned for your life. I wish I could tell you what it is, but just know you're destined for greatness."

This conversation happened again and again over the four years of my high school experience, and as unbelievable as it seemed, I always needed to hear it. For me, high school was lonely, full of people who were trying to find themselves and as a result, seemed like they had split personalities. One day someone would be friends with me, the next day, we weren't talking. One day, we would have lunch together, the next they would avoid me. It was troubling.

I would often eat my lunch in the newspaper room (I was on staff) because I knew no matter how fake or phony the people around me seemed, everything within the four walls of that newspaper space would be there for me. I only needed to reflect on my mom's encouragement, focus on what story I was going to have published next and day by day I found enough strength to make it.

I knew Jesus back then, but in the thick of thinking *"this world would be better off without me. I bet no one would even miss me if I was gone,"* it was often hard to hear Him. I know that amid my constant and seemingly relentless thoughts of suicide, God used my mom to speak over my life. He used her voice to share His encouragement and through her, He convinced me that life would get better, I only had to stick around long enough to see. Now that I am several years out of both high school and college, I can say that my mom was right and I am so grateful that God kept me from giving into the temptation to take my life.

Someone once said suicide is a permanent solution to a temporary problem and, in my opinion, that's pretty darn accurate. We get so bogged down in our current surroundings and circumstances that we start to develop a distorted perspective. We can't step back long enough to look beyond them. It's hard to see what others see when they tell us we're destined to do great things and believe life can't get any better or worse than "this."

When I was battling thoughts that the world would be better or at least indifferent if I had never existed, I had convinced myself it was time to leave this Earth behind. That's why I know the majority of winning the battle to overcome suicidal thoughts will be fought and won in your mind. Paul knew the power thoughts have in our lives. That's why he said in Philippians 4:8 (The Message), "Summing it all up friends, I'd say you'll do best by filling your minds and meditating on things true, noble, reputable, authentic, compelling, gracious - the best, not the worst, the beautiful, not the ugly, things to praise, not things to curse." You can be like I was in high school and continue to mull over how much the hurt hurts and how it never feels like your days get better, or you can take Paul's advice and think on things that are beautiful and praiseworthy.

If you decide right now to reflect on the positive no matter what hard times you face, you'll notice your dark thoughts will start to fade away. It won't always be easy, but by the power of Christ, it will always be doable and doing it is absolutely necessary because like my mom said, "this is not the end of your story."

It has been over seven years since I thought about taking my life and I know a huge factor in that was changing my surroundings. God granted me with friends who love deeply and see every part of me. I found a true sanctuary in the church and got myself plugged into a church family. They provide me with a space to belong and be transparent about how I'm feeling. They also provide me with a built-in support group that's constantly around to pray for me.

When you plug into something bigger than yourself, eternity becomes your new focus. You are able to help support the needs of others. You can provide words that are uplifting and you aren't discouraged by bad days because you know you can stand on the Lord's promises. John 16:33 (NASB) says "These things I have spoken to you, so that in Me you may have peace. In the world you have tribulation, but take courage; I have overcome the world." Keep pushing.

Action Steps

- Ask God to help you identify the areas of your life where you may be dealing with anger and pray over each one by name for 21 days

- Ask God to reveal a situation or person whom you need to forgive. Remember forgiveness is for you and not the other person, they may not even know you were hurt by them. If you're that someone, ask God to help you humble yourself and apologize so you may receive forgiveness. Then read more about Joseph's story of forgiveness (Genesis 37-50)

- Write out your biggest worries and declare that you will hand them over to God (Psalm 55:22).

- If have had thoughts of suicide, please talk to a school counselor, pastor or the National Suicide Prevention Lifeline at (800) 273-8255.

Professional Life

Would you believe me if I told you that God is interested in your job description? Not only that but He sees how you use your gifts or what you spend money on every day and he wants you to use them for Him? Many of us are guilty of qualifying these things as secular and deciding that we'll decide what's best for us in those areas.

We greatly limit both ourselves and God by doing this, because in essence we're telling God there are particular check boxes in life where His presence is needed. Blessings – check. Healing – check. Help with relationships – check. But we don't want Him to touch any areas of life where we have not expressly allowed Him.

What would it look like if you committed your schooling, finances and career placement to God? Not just the spiritual things? I believe you would experience favor like you've never seen. I also think you'll gain clearer direction for your decision making. In the next few chapters, we'll explore this reality.

Chapter 10

Living for God at School and on the Job

I am in the communications industry and I cannot count the number of occasions I used to wish God had called me to a full-time job in ministry. I felt individuals called to working in ministry had the clearest road map to reach those God wanted them to reach. I didn't feel like they battled with questions like *"Does God even care about what I'm doing?"* or *"Am I really in a place where God can use me?* because God was included in their job description. They were paid to tell people about Him.

I discovered quickly that even those in ministry aren't always aware of what God is doing. We see big time pastors and priests being thrown into jail for ungodly living and pastors whose jobs shift depending on their market. So our commitment to God cannot and should not rely on our job description. We must work to make as big an impact as we can in whatever amount of time God allots for a particular position because nothing in this life is permanent.

Colossians 3:23 (HCSB) says, "Whatever you do, do it enthusiastically, as something done for the Lord and not for men." Verse 24 goes on to say that when we do work as unto the Lord, we can be confident that we will receive a reward from Him when we get to heaven. Notice the verse says, "whatever you do" not "those things you feel like doing." Every chore around the house, every homework assignment, any job you may have on the side or the college internship all fall under this.

Each day we walk out of the doors of our houses, apartments or dorm rooms we should do so with the knowledge that we are Christ's representatives. If everyone in class gets the same homework assignment and you get a head start instead of complaining like the others, you're standing out from the crowd and someone is going to notice. If you clean your room and wash the dishes before your parents ask or help your roommate when they seem to be struggling, you're working as unto God and not men. If you stand up for the person who is bullied at your school or college, you're not only letting your light shine (Matthew 5:16), you're following a commandment. "Speak out on behalf of the voiceless and for the rights of those who are vulnerable." (Proverbs 31:8, CEB)

Every illustration mentioned opens up a door for you to share your faith with everyone you meet. It allows you to be God's witness and demonstrate that when people turn their lives over to Him, a change takes place.

If you are living out your faith and someone asks you about it, you can share with boldness and not have to worry about finding the right occasion to bring Christ up in conversation. What we do with our actions conveys more than we could ever say with our words. What are your actions at work, home, school and on your campus saying about the God you serve?

Action Steps

- Think about the areas in your life where you're working as unto men and not unto God.
- Write Colossians 3:23 on a notecard and tape it somewhere you can see it often so you will get daily motivation.
- Write down three ways you can let your light shine at school and on your job this week.

Chapter 11

Stay in Your Lane: The Importance of Operating in Your God-Given Gifts

If you have ever been to a kindergarten or elementary school play, you could agree that it's not uncommon to see something like "Tree #1" or "Chipmunk" on a cast sheet. If the theatrical production, *Romeo & Juliet*, had a tree as a part of the cast, it would be very strange for the tree to start quoting Juliet's lines.

Largely because the tree isn't supposed to be Juliet, it's supposed to be a tree and the director designed it that way when they did the casting. They weren't interested in why the tree felt Juliet was a better role, he or she was more concerned with the individual being the best tree they could be.

Although this illustration may seem silly, sometimes the tree in this story is no different from you and me. We look at the gifts God has given us and the roles He has assigned us and we decide there is something else we would rather be doing, as if in crafting our purpose, He made a mistake. It's just like in the previous chapter when I stated I used to wish God had called me to full-time ministry. I was making the assumption that I could better assess the role that was best for me.

Romans 9:20-21 (NLT) reads, "…Who are you to criticize God? Should the thing made say to the one who made it, 'Why have you made me like this?' When man makes a jar out of clay, doesn't he have a right to use the same lump of clay to make one jar beautiful, to be used for holding flowers, and another to throw garbage into?"

Now, of course, God doesn't use His children as garbage disposals, but this verse illustrates that when God has picked our purpose, we have to learn to bloom where we are planted. Although we may feel like our time is best spent somewhere else, we can see in Mark 5:18-20 that being obedient and responding to where God has called us can have benefits.

The verse reads, "While he was climbing into the boat, the one who had been demon-possessed pleaded with Jesus to let him come along as one of his disciples.

But Jesus wouldn't allow it. He says, "Go home to your own people, and report to them what great things the Lord has done for you and how He had mercy on you." (NASB). Before our key verse, Jesus has just cured this man from demon possession. We can understand why the man wanted to stick close to Jesus. He might have been thinking, "this guy knows where all the action is, I need to go wherever he's going." He was ready and willing to travel the seas, but Jesus denies him and says in verse 19, "Go home to your own people and tell them what the Lord has done for you."

I am sure you can empathize with the man's disappointment. Life with Jesus seemed way more adventurous than life back home and had the potential to result in more stories. But, instead of fighting Christ's commandment, the newly cured man was obedient to his calling. Mark 5:20 says, "He began to preach in the Ten Towns about what Jesus had done for him." The result: He was the talk of the town.

God may not send you abroad to share your testimony because your mission field is right where you are. There is someone in your life, in your extended family or in your circle who may not hear the Gospel unless you share it. So God wants you to stay in your lane, where all of your important work is located. You won't see everything God is doing in you right now, but the important part is that you give all you have got each day and let God do the rest. I know this can be hard to do, especially in a culture where everyone is constantly posting the great thing they did last weekend or where they are traveling next. But the truth of the matter is we all will have to stand on our own two feet on the day of of judgment (1 Corinthians 4:5) and God will not want to hear excuses about why we did not fulfill the roles He predestined for us.

Action Steps

- Ask God to help you stop comparing your calling to others. Pray that He'll help you to bloom where you are planted.
- Ask your friends and family what things you are really good at, there may be things you have failed to notice
- Write out your God-given gifts and note how you can start using them.

Chapter 12

Finances

I had sinned. As I sat in front of my computer staring at the red numbers that indicated overdraft fees. I realized that my overspending had caught up with me. Days passed and those numbers stayed red for over a week. It was embarrassing and it was shameful; but it forced me to recognize a harsh reality: I had allowed money to rule and I was serving it instead of it serving me.

Matthew 6:24 (NLT) says, "No one can serve two masters. For you will hate one and love the other; you will be devoted to one and despise the other. You cannot serve both God and money." You may think you could never be a servant to an object. If so, please allow me to give you some insight into the definition of a servant. A servant is a person who is devoted to or guided by something. This can take two distinct forms when it comes to money. You can become so consumed by debt or fearful of overspending that you will not justify spending anything. Or you may be so devoted to making money, you will do anything to get it, even if it's contrary to your beliefs. Either way you are serving money.

Many people, after having accumulated a lot of money, start to develop a problem with greed. The Bible gives many warnings: "Beware! Guard against every kind of greed. Life is not measured by how much you own." (Luke 12:15, NLT) So how can we avoid becoming servants or slaves to money? It starts with a commitment to four things: giving, budgeting, establishing benchmarks and remaining debt-free.

Giving

We are told in Malachi 3:10 that the Israelites, God's original chosen people, were under judgment from God because they had stopped giving their tithes. In Biblical times, people's tithes were often a portion of their harvest (grain, oil, seed, cattle, or other form of barter.). Today, tithes are most commonly associated with 10% of our earnings.

If we earn $150, a tithe to God would be $15. If we receive a $50 allowance from family, we would be responsible for giving God five dollars. We are supposed to submit our tithes to the church we attend since we can't mail God a check. This allows us to help fund the body of Christ and take part in whatever initiatives or missions that are associated with our church.

Giving is freeing for me because it's a constant reminder that nothing in my bank account is actually mine. It allows me to give to others in need because I can be a delivery person for someone else's blessing. When we tithe, we are showing God we understand all we have comes from Him. We also give Him the opportunity to bless our current circumstances and are trusting that He will make our ends meet. The end of Malachi 3:10 (NIV) says, "'Test me in this,' says the Lord Almighty 'and see if I will not throw open the floodgates of heaven and pour out so much blessing that there will not be enough room to store it.'"

Budgeting

The second way we can avoid becoming servants or slaves to money is through budgeting. Proverbs 27:23-24 says, "Know well the condition of your flock and pay attention to your herds for wealth is not forever, not even a crown lasts a lifetime." Before cash became a common form of currency, people would often trade or barter items like sheep and goats or grain for purchasing. When we read "keep well the condition of your flock," we can interpret that as "know where your money is going, keep track of everything."

Further support for budgeting can be found in Proverbs 21:5 (GNT). It reads "Plan carefully and you will have plenty; if you act too quickly you will never have enough." I remember reading that particular scripture and thinking, "the Bible talks about everything!" Christ knew it would be necessary to tell us to fight against impulse spending and advocate for budgeting because we know He supplies all our needs. The problem is we find ourselves always wanting the unnecessary.

We could have a fridge full of groceries and still complain about not having anything to eat. So, instead of working within our food budget, we spend above it by frequenting fast-food places. If it's not food, we may spend way too much of our budget on clothing - always on a mission to have the trendiest thing. That's why when we budget, it's important to pray that God will help us to be wise with our spending and decipher between a want and a need. James 1:5 says, "If any of you lacks wisdom, [you] should ask God who gives to all generously and without criticizing and it will be given to [you]."

I am not saying you can't have any fun when it comes to money. I have seen a number of people be able to vacation or be extremely generous with their gift giving and do it stress-free because they set the money aside, but you have got to stick to the amount of money you determined was responsible for your budget. If you set aside $50 for the month for entertainment, once your $50 is spent, that's got to be it. Dipping into other funds to cover unplanned expenses is a surefire way to get into debt. Take it from someone who has lived it.

Another mistake we sometimes make is spending money we haven't yet received. Those decisions sound something like, "well, I can't really afford this right now, but I get paid on Friday, so it will all balance out." Your next check isn't always guaranteed and it's better to wait until you have actually been paid so you don't have to do any guessing.

James 4:13-14 (ESV) says, "Come now, you who say, 'Today or tomorrow we will go into such and such a town and spend a year there and trade and make a profit' - yet you do not know what tomorrow will bring. What is your life? For you are a mist that appears for a little time and then vanishes." So when we spend money we haven't received yet, we're not only being poor stewards of our money but we are making the assumption that we'll be around to take care of the cost we created, taking no heed to the possibility of there being an emergency where we will really need that money.

When you are budgeting, you will want to make sure a portion of every check or allowance goes towards savings. Consider it your rainy-day fund for unexpected expenses that come your way, like needing to replace a tire or filling a medical prescription. You can have a separate savings fund for fun activities, such as the shopping spree you want to go on before your next family vacation or money to go towards homecoming or prom. Have no idea where to start with budgeting? There are a lot of budgeting templates you can access online for free.

Establishing Benchmarks

The next way we can avoid becoming servants to money is by establishing benchmarks. You may look at this word and get flashbacks of end-of-year testing, but financial benchmarks are points of reference that will help you measure the growth you have made in your finances.

Many of us have been guilty of only measuring how much we make has increased, but that is not a huge indicator of growth because we still might find ourselves living from paycheck to paycheck without the right budget. Deciding that we won't allow our income to dictate our spending allows us to make better choices in spite of our financial increase. When establishing your financial benchmarks ask yourself the following sample questions:

- Am I spending more or less since I've started budgeting?
- What are my top three areas of improvement?
- What is an area of weakness?
- How much money would I like to have in my savings in 90 days?
- What are some problem areas I have noticed while monitoring my spending?

It's hard to measure progress without taking time out to assess where you have been financially, where you are in this moment and where you're going. Establishing benchmarks will help you assess what needs adjusting and make changes where necessary.

Remaining Debt Free

If we are going to avoid becoming a servant to money, we must also be committed to being debt-free. Proverbs 22:7 (NLT) says, "Just as the rich rule over the poor, so the borrower is slave to the lender." As women in Christ, we should only be slaves to righteousness. Being weighed down by the chains of debt limits us from living out God's best. The $150 we spend each month trying to pay off a credit card expense could be used to feed the hungry, help the homeless or even a friend.

I pray that if you are reading this right now, you are already debt-free. If you're not, a family member may have gotten you set up with a credit card previously. While I know credit cards can be used to build credit, this only happens when cards are handled responsibly. The best piece of advice I have ever gotten when it comes to credit cards is that if you can't afford to purchase what you are thinking about buying with the money you have in your account, then you should not buy it on credit.

If you're going to buy on credit, only purchase gas (especially if you get cash-back for that type of purchase) and items that you can pay off in full before the end of the billing statement. Some use credit cards for emergencies but it's better to have your emergency fund in real money so you can take care of things swiftly and not be paying on an emergency six months from now.

Student loans are another huge source of debt for young people. Some ways to avoid falling into their trap are applying for scholarships and grants - neither require the money to be paid back. You can go to school in-state and avoid out-of-state fees, spend some time working and saving up for college, and look into schools that have work-study. Even if you're in college and have student loans already you can start paying on them now - setting aside a portion every week could greatly decrease the amount of interest you have to pay when you graduate. It's also important to keep applying for scholarships through all four years of college because some scholarships you may not have been eligible for as a freshman might be up for grabs when you're a sophomore or junior. Just do the proper research.

You can avoid becoming a servant to money, if you change the financial decisions you make today. I won't pretend that the four commitments I have listed in this chapter are an all-encompassing list of steps to financial success, but they will undoubtedly get you headed in the right direction.

Action Steps

- Start establishing a monthly budget
- Make a note of how your relationship with money changes when and if you start tithing
- Write out three financial benchmarks you want to reach in the next 30 days.

Physical Life

As a member of God's family and furthermore as women, people will pay a great deal of attention to our physical appearance. I believe this is because our outward appearance can sometimes be a big indicator of what's going on within.

Sleepless nights from not trusting in God, can lead to us to looking pale, frail and exhausted while trusting in Him and peaceful, restful sleep can lead to a glow in our skin. The proper nutrition can give us the strength to push through rigorous activity just as inconsistent fitness routines can lead to us feeling extremely lazy.

Just like in all the other areas of our life, when we submit our physical selves to Christ we allow Him to use us at our full capacity. This is important because we're told in 1 Corinthians 6:19 that our body is the temple of the Holy Spirit. With that fact in mind, let's look at some ways we can keep from neglecting the place He lives.

Chapter 13

Nutrition and Fitness

Imagine moving to a new place. Your heart is filled with anticipation, nervousness and excitement about the possibilities that lie within your new residence. Move-in day arrives and you and your parents drive up to this gorgeous three-story house with a beautiful front lawn and garden. They look back at you and say "This is where we'll be staying." You know you're going to love it and then...you walk in.

The inside is trashed. Paint is chipping off the walls, the space has a rodent problem and the stench is so awful you have to hold your breath. You were fooled by the house's outward appearance.

This happens far too often in our every day lives. We see people who are great looking but are rotting inwardly every day or even may be fighting off disease. We can't simply rely on good genes to get us where we're going, we must make sure that we are living clean.

Fighting the Myth

On my 24th birthday, one of my roommates at the time, Zuri, showed up to a picnic I was having and she was toting a grocery bag brimming with variety packs of chips and a family-sized package of Oreo cookies. Cookies and chips are my weakness, even though I didn't care much for them as a kid. I was able to munch liberally on what my roommate had brought because all of my guests were full by the time she arrived.

I continued to eat all of the junk-food leftovers once we were back at the house and for the next week and a half, no less than sixty-five percent of my meals included cookies and chips because of their availability. I learned a huge lesson: when it comes to eating healthy, a balanced diet starts at the grocery store.

Our youthfulness may lead us to believe we can eat anything, but it is really important to be conscious of what we put in our bodies. I can't say that one diet is more beneficial than the other. Gone are the days when certain foods were forbidden. Christ changed all that when he came to die for our sins. In the beginning of the New Testament, Christ talked to the Pharisees about this matter. They felt they were "holier" because they only ate the kind of food that was approved in the Old Testament, but Jesus quickly corrected them by saying in Matthew 15:11 (HCSB), "It's not what goes into the mouth that defiles a man but what comes out of the mouth, this defiles a man." I prefer to live by the "everything in moderation" lifestyle so I don't develop poor eating habits.

While you may feel like you can eat anything because of your youth, rest assured, that like all things we do, your eating habits will catch up with you. That's why if you establish healthy practices now while it's early, you can help improve your long-term health.

Meal Prepping

Meal preparation is an extremely helpful tool when you're trying to be intentional with your eating. You can suggest sitting down and planning your meals for the week before you and your folks or you and your roommates (if you do that together) go grocery shopping. This activity helps ensure that you buy all the ingredients needed for a particular dish. It also decreases the likelihood of getting fast food because "you don't have anything to eat."

For me, meal prepping typically involves a lot of grains and takes place on Sundays. After grocery shopping, I'll get out two big pots, one for pasta and one for rice, then look in my pantry for the different things I'd like to add to my grains. Sometimes I'll opt out on meat and fix corn, beans and broccoli to toss into my rice. Other times, if I want some protein I'll add chicken or turkey.

When I am preparing pasta, I use red sauce because I believe it reheats better than an Alfredo sauce, and I will toss in whatever veggies and meats suit me. I love separating my snacks into sandwich bags so they are easy to grab when I'm packing my lunch in the morning. Yes, I still pack my lunch ☺.

When I have finished cooking, I break out the plastic containers and separate my main dishes into proper portions and, voila, I've got food for the week. This helps reduce impulse spending and results in a healthy meal. Now, there are still days when I choose a night out to eat with friends or G instead of the meal that's patiently waiting in my fridge, but I only do this occasionally.

Get Up and Move Something

When it comes to exercising, a little physical activity can take you a long way. You don't need a fancy gym membership to do things like running in place, crunches, lunges, squats and other cardio exercises. I like working out at home so I can't use the excuse that I didn't have time to get to the gym. While I work out, I may listen to a twenty-five-minute podcast to keep my mind engaged while my body is working. I also really like watching fitness videos on YouTube. These make me feel like I'm getting the benefits of taking a structured class without having to leave my bedroom.

Some people find it helpful to schedule their workouts around areas on their body they want to target. For example, you may do cardio paired with arms and abs strength training on Monday, Wednesday and Friday. Tuesday and Thursday, you may do some cardio paired with strength training for your legs and back. This variety helps to avoid muscle fatigue. If you need a good starting point, check out these sample workouts.

Abs – three sets of 15
-   Plank (try to work up to 1 minute)
-   Crunches
-   Abdominal twists (this works your oblique muscles)

Legs – two sets of 15 per leg
-   Squats
-   Lunges
-   Wall Sits: 1 minute

- Calf raises

Back – two sets of 15 each

- Chin ups
- Hyper-extensions

Arms – two sets of 15 each

- Boxer punch
- Pushups (be sure to research the proper form! I'd been doing pushups wrong for years without knowing it
- Pull-ups
- Arm circles

When you feel like you have gotten the hang of it, add 5 more reps for each. I like to pair these exercises with a cardio activity like running, biking or even dancing! If you need the accountability of working out with a group, research free workout classes in your city.

Fitting It All In

As you review this chapter with all its mentions of workouts and meal prepping your mind may be consumed with one thing - time! The truth is, you won't find the time to put these practices in place, you will have to take the time you already have from some other activity. You could opt for working out for 30 minutes instead of hitting the snooze button on your alarm clock three times each morning. If you have breaks between classes, you could write out your grocery list for the week.

Once you make your physical life a priority, it becomes easier to nurture. Taking care of our physical bodies is essential for purpose-driven living because it enables us to serve the world around us more effectively and give us the energy we need to function. So both healthy eating and consistent physical activity necessary.

Action Steps

- Sit down with your family or roomies sometime this week and plan out your meals using an online meal planning worksheet

- Create a workout schedule highlighting areas you'd like to focus on over the next 21 days.

- Substitute one of your junk food items for something healthy for the next seven days (Ex: eat fresh strawberries instead of a pint of ice cream).

Chapter 14

Appearance

I have been involved with the teen ministry at my church in New Orleans for two years at the time of this book's publication and spending multiple days out of the week with my teen babies always makes me so happy. No matter if we're gathering at church or meeting out in the community, I am always conscious of how I present myself to the girls in the ministry because I know having more young women set an example for me when I was a teen would have had a tremendous effect on me. Also, I know my girls are always watching so for me, good presentation starts with clothing.

Preparation for an outing with my teens means a solid amount of time spent in my closet weighing the pros and cons of every outfit. I never pull out something I wouldn't want to see them in and I pay close attention to the length, cut and fit so I can show them you can look great without having to put everything on display or creating the idea that you're giving something away. Over time, if I notice I have been wearing a certain outfit less and less, I will give it away or sell it. I don't ever want there to be questionable clothing in my closet.

Some general rules I have found helpful are if your pants or skirts are tight, be sure to wear a looser-fitting top. If you have a tight top, wear loose bottoms. I have also noticed that even a long dress can look like a mini-skirt depending on the shoes you wear with it. We all can appreciate turning heads, but if what we wear causes others, especially men, to lose focus on what they're doing, it may be worth starting over again.

First Peter 3:3-4 (HCSB) says, "Your beauty should not consist of outward things like elaborate hairstyle and the wearing of gold ornaments or fine clothes. Instead, it should consist of what is inside the heart with the imperishable quality of a gentle and quiet spirit, which is very valuable in God's eyes." Remember, you can be the best looking person in the room, but God is more focused on what is inside of you so make sure you are giving fair attention to your heart and mind.

Makeup - Work it with a little or work it with a lot

Makeup and I had a weird relationship for a long time. I didn't have a desire to wear it and struggled to understand why some girls were so obsessed with it. It wasn't until after college that I started to appreciate the subtle enhancements makeup offers.

Still, when I wear makeup, I typically don't do much beyond foundation, mascara and filling in my eyebrows. On special occasions or if I just feel like getting dolled up for a day at the office, I might don a bold-colored lipstick. My sister, Brittany, on the other hand, goes all in and her makeup masterpieces are flawless. She always picks something that perfectly complements her outfit and she makes it look so effortless.

Whether you are more like Brittany or more like me, you must do what feels natural to you within the confines of the rules set by whoever takes care of you. If you're in college you will have to use your best judgment. Learning a new application trick is as simple as watching a video on YouTube. Just remember that you were created in God's image and in His eyes you are already perfect.

Hair - A Woman's Glory

This hair thing - my, my, my. I know sometimes maintaining our hair feels taking care of a baby, but its upkeep is a necessary evil. I went natural in 2012 and I loved the convenience that came along with doing the big chop. I barely had to comb my hair, keeping it conditioned was the main focus. But once my hair started growing, I second-guessed the whole natural thing. It required work and time I wasn't sure I felt like investing. It wasn't until I read in God's Word how a woman's hair is her glory (1 Corinthians 11:15) that I began to appreciate this "headache" God had given me. I started to pray for the energy and motivation to take better care of my hair and work to keep it healthy. I also began to embrace and appreciate protective styles like box braids, Havana twists and sew-ins. No matter if you're natural or have a relaxer, my biggest suggestions for keeping your hair healthy are:

1. Get your hair trimmed regularly.
2. Keep your hair conditioned (I try to deep-condition my hair at least once every two weeks).
3. Pay attention to the products you use.
4. Don't dry your hair with a towel. Use a T-shirt instead. This minimizes putting stress on your tresses.
5. Sleep on a satin pillow case at night.

Bottom line - God knows every inch of you. He is familiar with every kink and curl of your hair, every beauty mark, and the clothing you have in your closet. Never forget "people judge by the outward appearance, but the Lord looks at the heart," (1 Samuel 16:7b NLT). It's easier to honor God with your appearance when your beauty starts within. God's Word says in Proverbs 31:30 (HCSB), "Charm is deceptive and beauty is fleeting, but a woman who fears the Lord is to be praised." We want to be good steward of our body while continuing to grow spiritually every day. This is achieved through time in God's word, praying, confessing sin to others (James 5:16), serving those in our community, forgiving and monitoring our speech (Ephesians 4:29).

Action Steps

- Do an inventory on the items in your closet and commit to giving away or repurposing those items that are too tight, too short or too low-cut for your frame.
- Write a list of all your physical and spiritual attributes and praise God for them one by one.
- Ask God what parts of your inward appearance need a makeover

Chapter 15

Honoring God with our Bodies

She hadn't waited, so on their wedding night, the magic and newness she had expected to share from making love to her husband for the first time was replaced by monotony. Everything seemed like the same old routine and she could not understand what was missing.

While any number of women could tell this story from their personal perspective, I've shared it to give a glimpse into what many young Christian men and women are dealing with after they've given in to sexual sin.

When we look around at all of the sexualized shows, movies and advertisements, it doesn't take long to find major sources of temptation. To the average person, waiting until marriage to have sex has been chalked up as some old school way of thinking. But there was no time contingency in the Bible when God had Paul pen these words to the church of Corinth.

Paul says, "Run from sexual sin! No other sin as clearly affects the body as this one does. For sexual immorality is a sin against your own body." (1 Corinthians 6:18, NLT), We can continue on to verses 19 and 20 to find out what this means. The verses read, "Don't you realize that your body is the temple of the Holy Spirit, who lives in you and was given to you by God? You do not belong to yourself, for God bought you with a high price. So you must honor God with your body."

When Christ died on the cross for your sins and mine, he paid the ultimate price and God gave the ultimate sacrifice so that we might be able to spend eternity with Him in heaven. By accepting Christ as our Savior we receive a new inhabitant into our bodies, the Holy Spirit and when we commit sexual sin, we involve the Holy Spirit who lives within us. We're sinning against him.

As someone who has chosen to wait, I will occasionally hear people say to me, "I don't know how you do it. That couldn't be me." I find this response to my commitment frustrating because it seems to downplay two things – one God's original design for sex inside of marriage and two- the power of the Holy Spirit to help me. In 1 Corinthians 10:13 (ESV) says "No temptation has overtaken you that is not common to man. God is faithful, and He will not let you be tempted beyond your ability, but with the temptation he will also provide the way of escape, that you may be able to endure it. "

God knows denying our flesh is not an easy thing, so He gives us a promise that we will always have a way out if we yield to His leading. Many argue that if God did not want us to enjoy sex, He would not have made us sexual beings. This isn't completely wrong and the Bible does not say to not have sex at all. God's request is that we engage in sex within the boundaries He has set. If we take the time to really dig into how God designed sex to function, it becomes easier to follow His directions for it.

J. Robin Maxson and Garry Friesen, in their book, Singleness, Marriage and the Will of God,[9] cite three main purposes that are fulfilled when we follow the biblical design for sex inside of marriage. The first is procreation. We are told in Genesis 1:28 "be fruitful and multiply." Separating sex and reproduction treats sex as a mere physical act and not a purposeful one. Naturally, not every sexual encounter will result in children, but marriage creates an inviting space to welcome them. It gives stability that may not have otherwise been present.

Psalm 127:3 says, "Children are a gift from the Lord, they are a reward from him." You can see how this view drastically opposes secular society's view on sex as some regard children to be an accident or result from not taking the proper precautions.

The next purpose Maxson and Friesen state as being fulfilled in marital sex is a one-flesh union. Genesis 2:18 (NLT) reads, "Then the Lord God said, 'It is not good for man to be alone. I will make a helper who is just right for him.'" God pulled Eve from Adam's rib and by bringing the couple back together, provided completeness. Friesen says, "in sex, we move beyond ourselves - joining back together the union that was severed."

The third purpose of marital sex, according to Maxson and Friesen, is illumination. When experienced inside the marital covenant, sex is the closest mirror image we will ever get to the Trinity relationship shared by God the Father, Christ the Son and the Holy Spirit. We are able to gain a deeper understanding of what it means to be one with another person. The book's authors note that "sex does not just engage our bodies; it also touches our souls." This is why many times it can be hard to break off a relationship when two people have engaged in premarital sex. It's like gluing two pieces of cardboard together and trying to separate them. A trace of each piece will still be found on the other half.

Just like victory over anger, unforgiving spirits, and thoughts of suicide, the victory to overcoming sexual temptation begins in our heads. We must greet each day and each interaction with a determined spirit to stay on top of our thoughts and keep them in line with what God says. Second Corinthians 10:5 says, "Take captive every thought and make it obedient to Christ" and Romans 3:15 says, "Put on the Lord Jesus Christ and make no provision for the flesh to arouse its desires."

I made a commitment as a teen that I would not have sex before marriage but the temptation to break that promise to both God and myself was constantly present. When pre-marital sex started to seem appealing to me, I had to take a step back and look at what stimulants were contributing to that feeling. I realized the music I was listening to and the shows I was watching made it hard not to fantasize about the kinds of things I thought I would enjoy physically. Something that helped me give these things up was the old adage that says, "You are what you eat." The same is true for our spiritual bodies.

If we fill our hearts and minds with images that cause us to lust after our brothers in Christ, we are setting ourselves up for failure, but if we fill our hearts and mind with God's Word and stay in tune with what He would want, it becomes a lot easier to fight against temptation. Once I adjusted the kind of music I listened to and what I was watching, I was able to stay on track. I also spent time reading things like Singleness, Marriage and the Will of God so that I was constantly reminding myself that this was not just some empty promise I made, it was a fiery determination to enjoy sex God's way.

Geordan, was just as committed as I was to abstaining from sex. Some days, we would pray together for the strength to abstain and God helped us to be honest with one another when we felt like a slip up was in the realm of possibility.

I felt like this made us closer and allowed our relationship to deepen. It made it so I began to view sex as an enhancement to what God was already helping us establish. If you know you have a problem with lust, ask God to point out the influences. Maybe it isn't TV and music, maybe it's the books you read or the people you hang with.

Align yourself with young women who share your commitment to abstinence because being the only one not talking about sex can be a struggle. This is especially important if you're in college and have a lot of free time on your hands. If you have already engaged in sex, you can start over again.

You are worth waiting for my love, and so is your future husband.

Action Steps

- Write down some things you could cut out of your day that may be contributing to your temptation to have sex before marriage.
- Pray over these items and ask God to reveal the top priority for your life.
- Spend some time meditating on Philippians 4:8 and 2 Corinthians 10:5.

Recreational Life

Our free time or "recreation" is another segment of life we convince ourselves God has nothing to do with. As long as we're going to church and praying every now and then, why should He care about what we do with the rest of our time, who we choose as friends or even with whom we decide to be romantic?

The answer is, He cares because we are His children. In the same way our parents share their opinions on how we spend our time, who we choose as friends and with whom we decide to be romantic, God seeks to chime in because all of these pieces make a great difference in who we are. If we are going to be reflections of Him, then He must be included in how we manage them.

Chapter 16

A Lesson in Time Management

Time - one of our most precious assets. Once it's gone we cannot get it back. You might think this would lead us to guard it with the utmost diligence but far too often, we engage in activities that waste it.

North Point pastor, Andy Stanley, broke down two truthful concepts in his Bible study, *Time of Your Life*.[8] The first said that there is a cumulative value to investing small amounts of time in certain activities over a long period of time and the second said there is no cumulative value for the random things we opt for over the important things in our lives.

He believed if we were to add up all the random things we choose every day over the important things we know we should be doing; the sum would be zero. As I listened to this, I felt instant guilt over all the time I wasted in the previous week:

- Choosing ten more minutes of sleep over an extra ten minutes in prayer before starting my day.
- Choosing to be on time to a casual outing instead of enjoying one-on-one time with Geordan.
- Purchasing fast food because it was quick instead of investing an extra twenty minutes to make a meal that would last for a couple days.

It is easy to look at any of those items individually and say they are not a big deal, but in the long term, all of our decisions either have huge dividends or major consequences. The ten minutes of extra sleep we opt for in the morning can turn into thirty minutes. Starting off the day with prayer and a commitment to fulfill God's will at the beginning of each day is better than opening each day flustered and irritated because of oversleeping.

Caring about our boyfriends or family or husbands should take top priority over rushing them so we can be on time to a casual outing. Constant fast-food runs can lead to health issues and spending money on unnecessary things can cause problems with our finances. We can avoid all these things by learning to manage our time wisely. The key is making God a priority.

It may take some to-do list revamping and it may take resetting the alarm to an earlier time each morning, but

God sees those small sacrifices and the good news is He rewards those who seek Him.

Sometimes we fall victim to the belief that if we don't do something the moment we're thinking about it, it won't get done. I'm particularly guilty of this and every so often I look up and realize when I've put God on the back burner and turned myself over to the more tangible things demanding my attention.

Should I completely shirk my responsibilities and spend all day every day closed in my house talking to God instead? Of course not, that would be silly. It just makes far more sense to implement a system of organization so that I can handle things effectively and make sure to give God the time He wants with me.

The Bible says, "So be careful how you live. Don't live like fools, but like those who are wise. Make the most of every opportunity in these evil days. Don't act thoughtlessly, but understand what the Lord wants you to do." (Ephesians 5:15-17, NLT).

When we start our day consulting with our Divine Designer on how our hours should be spent and then seek out those things we believe He would deem worthy of our time, it's easier to avoid getting sidetracked. We may only spend two minutes each checking Twitter, Snapchat, or Instagram, but two minutes multiplied by three is six and if we check ten times a day, then a whole hour that could have been spent investing in Kingdom building, learning, encouraging or connecting with someone face-to-face no longer exists. Do not fall victim to this, decide at the beginning of the day how much time you want to dedicate tor each item on your to-do list.

While I was writing this book and not until I was finished, I set my alarm for 5 a.m. I had an allocated amount of time set aside for Bible study, writing, web development, social media management and exercise. Doing this helped me to feel confident in my time management skills. Any day I opted to sleep in, I'd feel like so much time had been wasted. I chose to invest small amounts of time in things that were worthwhile and fought the temptation to give into what felt easy. As I developed that discipline, I was able to enjoy the peace that comes at the end of each day that I've chosen to spend wisely.

Action Steps

- Think of some new ways you can start living wisely.
- Make note of what takes up most of your time, it will help reveal your priorities.
- Make adjustments as necessary

Chapter 17

Choosing Your Circle

In college I went through several friend group transitions and I think a big part of it tied into not really knowing what I wanted out of a friend. Many friendships were formed simply because of the person's proximity to my dorm room or shared classes, but the ones that lasted were built on similar interests, priorities and motivations.

All but a few people in my current circle of friends have a relationship with Christ and strong family ties. I did not know it then, but these two pillars would become crucial in building friendships as I moved away from my best friends after graduating from college in Columbia, Missouri and was tasked with finding even more friends in New Orleans.

There were times after I moved to New Orleans when people questioned why I didn't smoke or drink. It was not a sufficient reason in their eyes that it was a lifestyle choice based on my faith but for some this wasn't sufficient reasoning. I didn't have anything to hide, I just knew those habits wouldn't reflect Christ in me. So time with that particular group of people subsided and I spent time alone with Christ or with people who accepted me for me.

First Corinthians 15:33 (HCSB) says, "Do not be deceived: Bad company corrupts good morals." If we are going to lead a Christian lifestyle marked by purposeful living, we must dedicate ourselves to finding a solid community. After throwing myself a pity party from having to pass on particular outings, I prayed that God would send me friends who would give me advice inspired by the Holy Spirit. Friends who would fast and pray with me, with whom I could join in ministry, friends who did not criticize me for saying no or understood that there were certain shows I had to abstain from watching. And you know what? God provided them for me through the members of my church family.

Some people don't think highly of the church, but I am here to tell you, as a young Christian woman, you cannot truly thrive without it. Just like our hand would cease to function if it was cut off from the body we we cease to truly function when we are cut off from Christ's body (the church). We should look forward to time we get to spend with our brothers and sisters in Christ because we need them. Hebrews 10:24-25 (HCSB) says, "And let us be concerned about one another in order to promote love and good works, not staying away from our worship meetings, as some habitually do, but encouraging each other, and all the more as you see the day [when Christ comes back] drawing near."

Inside of God's family we're able to discover more about ourselves and contribute more to Kingdom building. We can't cut church out of the equation if we're serious about growing because the church is Christ's bride (Ephesians 5:25).

Can you imagine what it would be like if your dad had a friend that came over all the time and said, "Hey man, I love you and appreciate spending time with you, but your wife is annoying, unwanted and unnecessary." That would be extremely disrespectful and your dad would probably kick that so-called friend out of the house.

It's the same with God, we can't say we love Him and then in the same breath talk about why we hate the church and avoid His children. Some of my favorite things about having my church friends who have become more like family is that I can cry with them, I can confess my sin to them (James 5:16), I can acknowledge my failures and weaknesses without having to deal with questions like "Why are you struggling if you're supposedly a

Christian?" We're able to hold each other accountable and provide a word of encouragement sent from the Holy Spirit because we're all plugged into Him and there's something special about the transparency we share amongst each other.

As my relationships with my friends grew, I was introduced to more and more people who looked like me and had the same passion for ministry. My eyes had been opened up to this entirely new population of twenty-somethings who were bold in their love for Christ and dedicated to serving him fully.

Having this friend group showed me if we are determined to live on purpose, the people we choose to live life with will be important. Our actions and habits are greatly affected when we are not connected to fellow believers who share our spiritual needs and convictions.

There may be times when you feel like you're the only young person at your school, on your job, at your house or even on this planet who is trying to live for Christ. You may have started to believe your college campus is the headquarters for debauchery because everyone is so focused on living liberally. Be encouraged, if you pray for Christian friends, God will send them. Do not fall for the myth that there aren't any young people living for Christ, and don't become so disillusioned that you believe you can just wait to live for him when you're older and have gone through more experiences.

Be bold enough to ask God to surround you with individuals now who will help you grow spiritually and be patient enough to wait on the people who are headed your way even if you can't see them coming.

Please understand, this chapter is not about only having Christian friends. If you did that, it would be hard to fulfill The Great Commission we discussed in the chapter about discipleship. I have some very close friends who are non-believers and getting to talk with them regularly encourages me because I know God can create a bridge from my heart to theirs because of our already established relationship. Rick Warren, the pastor of Saddleback Church in Lake Forest, California, says you can't win your enemies to Christ, you can only win your friends but you still must be diligent in your selection.

Choose people who will help you stand against the lure of your temptations. Ecclesiastes 4:9-10 (NLT) says, "Two people are better off than one, for they can help each other succeed. If one person falls, the other can reach out and help. But someone who falls alone is in trouble. "Don't set yourself up to fall alone.

We serve a God who understands the importance of community so much that He built one in through our faith family. As we continue to grow and expand our circle, we must be conscious of ensuring that there are enough people in it who we know will help keep us on the path of purposeful living.

Action Steps

- Take inventory of your friendships - ask yourself which ones are in order with your Christian walk.
- Pray for the strength to distance yourself from friends who may be corrupting your character.
- Pray that God will send Christian friends your way

Chapter 18

Romantic Relationships

Want to know a secret? I didn't get my first kiss until I was 18 and I was 21 before I had a boyfriend. Given that my then boyfriend is now husband, I can't say I regret the delay. But trust me, I had many a moment with God in the midst of His preservation process when I asked Him "Who am I waiting for?" or "Is there anyone out there for me?"

I had a conversation with my mom when I was 16 about how I wouldn't date anyone who didn't "bring anything to the table." I wasn't interested in the guy whose first move was to tell me I was pretty; my dad could do that and did so regularly.

I also wasn't interested in some kind of parrot who only repeated my words back to me and didn't actually have any original thoughts of their own. Boring! I wanted a man who would complement me not complete me, a man who inspired and challenged me to think about things differently. I wanted someone who was all the things it was hard for me to be (i.e. quiet, patient, still) and though it took what seemed like forever, that is who God sent me.

There was a time when my so-called requirements were a lot different. I wanted whoever God sent me to be athletic, have green eyes, be a good singer and be enamored with me. As I matured, however, I focused less on physical appearance and spent more time reflecting on the list of characteristics I wanted my future husband to possess. I wrote down things like God-fearing, respectful, someone who was proud of me, someone I could be proud of, someone who was good with children, patient, had a strong connection to family and was a good listener.

You know what's funny? Geordan doesn't match up with anything on my list of physical "requirements" (he's extremely good looking, just not in the way I was expecting) but he is the embodiment of every single item I had written on my character traits list before I ever met him. The truth that "people judge by the outward appearance, but the Lord looks at the heart," (1 Samuel 16:7b, NLT) was confirmed through our first interaction. I read once that marriage wasn't designed to make us happy, but to make us holy and I couldn't really understand it. Now as I reflect on the past few years Geordan and I have been together, I can see the ways I have become holier because of our relationship.

For example, as I mentioned in Chapter Nine, I used to have a problem with anger. In the beginning, I would blame G for "making me angry," but over time I began to understand that he simply helped bring up what had already been brewing under the surface. When I was able to admit that I did have anger issues God started working on them and He used Geordan to balance out my "passion" with patience.

Patience is another attribute I have acquired since being with Geordan. I am really big on being timely and sometimes, not doing so makes me anxious. G has more of a go with the flow type attitude and that used to drive me crazy. I still plan, presently, but I have learned to let God do more of the guiding and I have become drastically aware that I am operating on His timing. That means even when I plan something seamlessly, if God doesn't approve of it, it may not take place. With my newfound patience, I have learned to wait on what He has for me.

One last thing I want to share in how my relationship with G has helped make me holy is that I learned something crazy about love. It's a choice. Not an emotion. If it were an emotion, why would there be so many verses in the Bible commanding us to do it?

Not only that, but if love were an emotion, how could Christ cite love of the Lord and loving our neighbors as the most important commandment in Matthew 22:38? It wouldn't make sense.

When things got tough in the beginning stages of Geordan and my relationship I was ready to call it quits but God quickly showed me that is not how love functions. If I say I want to be with Geordan and have made the choice to love him, then I must put in the work necessary to make sure that love continues to flourish.

That's why many wedding vows give the conditions "for better, for worse, for richer, for poorer, in sickness and in health, to love and to cherish, 'til death do us part." That's how Christ loves us, so of course it reflects how he want us to love each other.

If you are reading this and thinking "I'm not in a relationship right now, none of this applies to me" or "I'm good Brie, I'm just waiting on Mr. Right to present himself to me," let me say while I don't know anyone who would turn their nose up to being swept off their feet, it's important not to be so eager to jump in a relationship with the first guy who tells you you're pretty.

If you're dating, do so intentionally. Date someone who will help you grow spiritually. Date someone who will help you become holy and as you get older, date someone you can see yourself marrying. Seek out the kinds of relationships grounded in mutual interests, enjoyment of each other's company and understanding that keeping Christ as the focus will help you push through your rainy days. If you're not dating, don't rush that time away. When your man shows up, you will want to be ready.

Paul says in 1 Corinthians 7:32a that an unmarried [person] can spend his time doing the Lord's work and thinking how to please Him. So make God your focus during this time period, confident that if you have the desire to be in a relationship, God will fulfill it in His timing. "Do no stir up or awaken love until the appropriate time." (Solomon 8:4, HCSB). When it comes, you'll know it.

Action Steps

- Start praying for your husband. I know this may seem crazy, but before Geordan and I ever met, I wrote letters to my future husband. This helped free my mind of certain thoughts or anxieties and it was special when I was finally able to share the letters with him. You can also ask God if marriage is even in His plans for your life.

- If you have a list of physical attributes for your future man, try and add in some spiritual assets you know the Lord would be pleased with. Pray for help if you need it.
- Write out ways a God-led relationship could help you become holier

Part 3:

Performing in Your Purpose

"So it is a sin for the person who knows to do what is good and doesn't do it."
James 4:17 (HCSB)

Whenever I have been hit with a lot of information, I usually have to take a step back and write out some action steps (as I've done with all the chapters in this publication). If I don't, it's hard to feel like I've truly gotten anything out of the experience and I risk not doing anything with the new knowledge I have been given.

We have covered a lot in this book and I want to make sure that as you finish it, you do so with the intention and ability to apply these practices. Truly living for God revolves around knowing the things you should do and then making the bold choice to do them.

Does that mean it will be easy? Not at all. But the Lord rewards those who follow His direction and you must trust that the way you live your life will inspire others to action.

Chapter 19

What's Next?

The road to purposeful living is laid out clearly in God's Word, but He does not and will not force us to live by it. Our lives here on Earth are a series of choices and choosing Christ as your Savior is a critical one if you are committed to living your life on purpose.

If you grasp nothing else from the book, please grasp this: purposeful living starts with God and is found only in Him. Anytime you seek fulfillment or meaning from your status, relationships, wealth, health, looks or anything else, you will wind up disappointed.

Everything we have highlighted in this book - your spiritual life, emotional life, professional life, physical life and recreational life can be used for God's glory. You simply have to submit those areas to Him.

You were built for God's pleasure, that's why He made you in His image. Allow yourself to live in fellowship with Him. Tap into your talents and spiritual gifts, all the while praying that He will direct you on how to use them. Pray that you become more like Christ through the transformative power of the Holy Spirit and live out the Great Commission. Throughout our time together, we have taken a look at some helpful choices you can make if you are determined to live a life that pleases God but whether you choose to apply them will be your decision.

When we started, I encouraged you to only read a chapter each day to help with application. The great part is, you now have this book as a resource and can review it as much as needed when you find yourself lacking direction. I have even put the action steps from each section at the back of the book for quick reference. It's my hope that you will take these words to heart and prayerfully go out and share them with your friends. Most of all I hope, that through reading this book, you feel like you have a better grasp on what it means to live your life on purpose.

Action Steps
- Review the action steps at the back of the book
- Create a three-point plan highlighting the three items you want to make your focus
- Pray that God will equip you to live out His purpose

Conclusion
Standing on God's Promises

It was the summer after I graduated from college and I was preparing to move to Miami for 10 months as a corps member for a federally funded organization. I had made plans to attend Florida International University after my service year was complete to obtain my Master's in International Business.

Just two weeks before I was set to go to Miami, I received a call from the New Orleans branch of the organization with whom I'd be serving. They needed me. Programming was scheduled to start in five days and they didn't have the staff necessary to function efficiently.

This threw me for a loop. I had all these perfectly laid plans that went out the window with one call from New Orleans. I called my mom to explain my distress, and she simply said, "Make new plans."

With that said, I prepared to move down to New Orleans. Keep in mind this was a city I had not even visited, much less lived in. I didn't know it at the time, but it would present me with a huge opportunity to grow in my faith and to be connected to fellow believers my age. It also became the birthplace of a new phase of my relationship with Geordan. It's where we got engaged.

New Orleans was where I learned about marketing and it was the place I learned to design websites from scratch. It's safe to say the city's entrepreneurial spirit and general 'go-getedness' inspired something within me and God used the skills I'd practiced in my marketing firm to land me a full-time job with a wonderful company. I can never forget that New Orleans is the place where God gave me the vision for *The Black Girl's Guide to Living on Purpose.*

All of this started with a leap of faith and none of the big things happened instantly. I spent the first four months after moving to New Orleans, asking God what He planned to do with me. I was confused and frustrated. I felt like I had no sense of direction beyond understanding this was where God had called me to be.

As I looked for encouragement in God's Word, I found a promise He'd given me in Philippians 1:6 (NLT) "And I am certain that God, who began the good work in you, will continue his work until it is finally finished on the day when Christ Jesus returns." He also gave that promise to you.

Dear sister, as you finish this book, I have to give you fair warning. Letting God use you is a scary thing. It requires trusting Him and not leaning on your own understanding (Proverbs 3:5). It means hard days and confusion will be a reality. You won't wake up every morning and know exactly what God will bring to you or that you will push through each moment with the highest confidence that you know what you're doing. What does come guaranteed with this life is peace. The pressure to have everything figured out is off of you because you can trust God to guide your footing (Psalm 119:105).

With God, you will experience some things beyond your wildest dreams. We're told in Ephesians 3:20 (HCSB) that God "is able to do above and beyond all that we ask or think according to the power that works in us." So you can trust that whatever vision you have for your life, God will expand in ways you never imagined.

First Corinthians 2:9 (NLT) says "No eye has seen, no ears heard, and no mind has imagined what God has prepared for those who love Him." I pray that this book has given you the motivation you need to hold on to that promise. Remember, God knew what He had planned for your life before you even existed.

My prayer is that whatever feelings of inferiority you may have had before reading this book, whatever thoughts that you don't matter and confusion about why you are here has decreased remarkably if not vanished, as you've sought God about all He has predestined. Your worth is rooted in who God designed you to be, and as you continue to make new discoveries, you should find yourself greeting each day expecting new opportunities.

It's time to go live out your purpose.

Action Steps in Review

If you're going to live your spiritual life on purpose

- Take The Smalley Institute's personality assessment online at http://www.smalley.cc/personality-quiz
- Try to guess the personalities of your friends
- Discuss the strengths and weaknesses that each of your personality types possess
- Make note of your passion a.k.a. the thing that "breaks your heart."
- Brainstorm ideas for how you can help solve the issue.
- Research the kinds of solutions people with your similar passions have created.
- Take a spiritual gifts test online at spiritualgiftstest.com
- Encourage one of your close friends to take it with you and discuss your similarities and differences.
- Talk to a leader at your church about the results and ask what ministries might benefit most from your spiritual gifts.
- If you want to know more about Christ so you can stand firmly on what you believe, spend some

time in the Gospels of Matthew, Mark, Luke and John.

- If you have studied for yourself, but are still having a hard time getting into this "follower of Christ" thing, read the book of James. James was Jesus' half-brother and was one of his biggest critics, but it took one encounter after Christ was raised from the dead for James to become a proclaimer of the Gospel.
- If you are ready to accept Jesus Christ as your Savior, follow the ABCs to salvation:
- Admit that you are a sinner and want to turn away from your sins (Romans 3:23, Romans 6:23, 1 John 1:9)
- Believe that Jesus Christ died on the cross for your sins and rose again on the third day (John 3:16, Romans 5:8)
- Confess that Jesus is now Lord over your life (Romans 10:9)
- Spend some time reviewing the model prayer in Matthew 6:9-13.
- Set an alarm to help make prayer a part of your daily routine.

- Start keeping a journal of things you have prayed for and mark when your prayers have been answered.

- Try putting your phone on airplane mode this evening before you go to sleep and fight the urge to look at it first thing in the morning.

- Spend some time using the Daily Docket, available at theartofsimple.net for a week and journal about any changes you see in your productivity.

- Read Luke 5 and pay special attention to verses 15-16. Jesus was very busy but he still had his priorities straight.

- Be honest with yourself about the things that may have replaced God on the throne of your heart

- Think through ways you can worship God through your time, money and energy today

- Allow God to reveal what things in your life may be preventing you from worshipping

- Look for opportunities for discipleship to help build up fellow believers and witness to nonbelievers.

- Try to establish a Paul, Barnabas and Timothy model - someone you can look to for spiritual advice, someone on your level and someone to disciple (teach).

- Start or join a small group so talking about your faith can become more natural

If you're going to live your emotional life on purpose

- Ask God to help you identify the areas of your life where you may be dealing with anger and pray over each one by name for 21 days
- Ask God to reveal a situation or person whom you need to forgive. Remember forgiveness is for you and not the other person, they may not even know you were hurt by them. If you're that someone, ask God to help you humble yourself and apologize so you may receive forgiveness. Then read more about Joseph's story of forgiveness (Genesis 37-50)
- Write out your biggest worries and declare that you will hand them over to God (Psalm 55:22).
- If have had thoughts of suicide, please talk to a school counselor, pastor or the National Suicide Prevention Lifeline at (800) 273-8255.

If you're going to live your professional life on purpose

- Think about the areas in your life where you're working as unto men and not unto God.
- Write Colossians 3:23 on a notecard and tape it somewhere you can see it often so you will get daily motivation.
- Write down three ways you can let your light shine at school and on your job this week
- Ask God to help you stop comparing your calling to others. Pray that He'll help you to bloom where you are planted.
- Ask your friends and family what things you are really good at, there may be things you have failed to notice
- Write out your God-given gifts and note how you can start using them in your profession
- Start establishing a monthly budget
- Make a note of how your relationship with money changes when and if you start tithing
- Write out three financial benchmarks you want to reach in the next 30 days

If you're going to live your physical life on purpose
- Do an inventory on the items in your closet and commit to giving away or repurposing

those items that are too tight, too short or too low-cut for your frame.

- Write a list of all your physical and spiritual attributes and praise God for them
- Ask God what parts of your inward appearance need a makeover
- Write down some things you could cut out of your day that may be contributing to your temptation to have sex before marriage.
- Pray over these items and ask God to reveal the top priority for your life.
- Spend some time meditating on Philippians 4:8 and 2 Corinthians 10:5.

If you're going to live your recreational life on purpose

- Think of some new ways you can start living wisely.
- Make note of what takes up most of your time, it will help reveal your priorities.
- Make adjustments as necessary
- Take inventory of your friendships - ask yourself which ones are in order with your Christian walk.
- Pray for the strength to distance yourself from friends who may be corrupting your character.

- Pray that God will send Christian friends your way
- Start praying for your husband. I know this may seem crazy, but before Geordan and I ever met, I wrote letters to my future husband. This helped free my mind of certain thoughts or anxieties and it was special when I was finally able to share the letters with him. You could also ask God if marriage is even in His plans for your life.
- If you have a list of physical attributes for your future man, try and add in some spiritual assets you know the Lord would be pleased with. Pray for help if you need it.
- Write out ways a God-led relationship could help you become holier

Index

1. "New Raw Video Shows Girl Assaulted and Thrown to Floor by Ben Fields, School Resource Officer (SC)," YouTube Video, 1:20 posted by Mars Daniels on October 27, 2015, https://www.youtube.com/watch?v=-QXqD2HsxAQ

2. Michael E. Miller "As death threats spread fear at Mizzou professors asks students to defeat 'bullies' and attend class." Last modified November 11, 2015. https://www.washingtonpost.com/news/morning-mix/wp/2015/11/11/as-threats-spread-fear-at-mizzou-a-professor-asks-students-to-defeat-bullies-and-attend-class/

3. John Schuppe, "The Death of Sandra Bland: What We Know So Far" Last modified July 23, 2015. http://www.nbcnews.com/news/us-news/death-sandra-bland-what-we-know-so-far-n396036

4. Kimberlé Williams Crenshaw with Priscilla Ocen and Jyoti Nanda, "The Hidden Toll of Race on Black Girls: What the Data Suggest," *Black Girls Matter: Pushed Out, Overpoliced and Underprotected*. (© 2015 African American Policy Forum): 17

5. Smalley Institute. Free Personality Test. http://www.smalley.cc/free-personality-test/

6. Gary D. Smalley, *The Five Love Languages: Singles Edition,* (Northfield Publishers 2009) 87

7. Tsh Oxenreider, "The Daily Docket," theartofsimple.net, http://creativecommons.org/licenses/by-nd/3.0/us/#

8. Andy Stanley, *Time of Your Life,* RightNow Media video, Session 3 (North Point Resources, 2012). https://www.rightnow.org/Content/Series/149#3

9. J. Robin Maxson and Garry Friesen, *Singleness, Marriage and the Will of God* (Oregon, Harvest House Publishers, 2012) 193-197

About the Author

Brieanna Daniels (known as Brie to her friends and family) is first and foremost a daughter of the King. Her faith in God is the guiding force in her life and she loves to share the message of Christ with everyone  she meets. Brie is a major foodie and resides in New Orleans where she serves in teen ministry. Brie is a 2013 graduate of the University of Missouri where she met her husband "G." When Brie is not writing you can find her reading a good book, finding cheap flights for her next adventure, eating a delicious meal or hanging with friends and family. To read more from Brie and to join the online Black Girls with Purpose community, visit blackgirlswithpurpose.org.

Did you enjoy this read? Be sure to leave a review on Amazon.com.

Made in the USA
Charleston, SC
07 March 2017